WAS JESUS GOD?

WAS JESUS GOD?

Richard Swinburne

OXFORD

UNIVERSITY PRESS

OXFORD

UNIVERSITY PRESS

Great Clarendon Street, Oxford OX2 6DP

Oxford University Press is a department of the University of Oxford.
It furthers the University's objective of excellence in research, scholarship,
and education by publishing worldwide in

Oxford New York

Auckland Cape Town Dar es Salaam Hong Kong Karachi
Kuala Lumpur Madrid Melbourne Mexico City Nairobi
New Delhi Shanghai Taipei Toronto

With offices in

Argentina Austria Brazil Chile Czech Republic France Greece
Guatemala Hungary Italy Japan Poland Portugal Singapore
South Korea Switzerland Thailand Turkey Ukraine Vietnam

Oxford is a registered trade mark of Oxford University Press
in the UK and in certain other countries

Published in the United States
by Oxford University Press Inc., New York

© Richard Swinburne 2008

The moral rights of the author have been asserted
Database right Oxford University Press (maker)

First published 2008

British Library Cataloguing in Publication Data

Data available

Library of Congress Cataloging in Publication Data

Data available

Typeset by Laserwords Private Limited, Chennai, India
Printed in Great Britain
on acid-free paper by
CPI Antony Rowe, Chippenham, Wiltshire

ISBN 978–0–19–920311–6

1 3 5 7 9 10 8 6 4 2

ACKNOWLEDGEMENTS

I am most grateful to two Oxford University Press readers, to the OUP philosophy editor Peter Momtchiloff, and to my daughter Nicola, for very helpful comments on an earlier version of the book. Thanks to Oxford University Press for permission to reuse much material already published in some of my longer books. And thanks too once again to Sarah Barker for all her patient typing and retyping.

R.S.

CONTENTS

INTRODUCTION

Are there good reasons for believing that there is a God? I have argued elsewhere, and especially in my book *Is There a God?*, that the general character of the natural world (and in particular the fact that it is governed by laws of nature which lead to the evolution of human beings) makes it probable that there is a God. But why should we suppose that God (if there is a God) is the Christian God? I plan to answer that question in this book and to show that, if there is a God, then the main doctrines which the Christian Church teaches about God, the doctrines which are special to Christianity and distinguish it from other religions which also claim that there is a God, are very probably true. Since the most important thing which Christians believe about God is that, while remaining God, he acquired a human nature and lived on earth for thirty years as a human being, Jesus Christ, I have called this book *Was Jesus God?* This book can be read as a sequel to *Is There a God?* or independently of it.

PART I

GOD LOVES US

1 GOD

I assume in this book that, on the basis of evidence such as the general character of the natural world or a person's own religious experience, there is a moderate probability that there is a God of the kind worshipped by Christians, Jews, and Muslims. (I emphasize the 'moderate'. I am not even assuming that the existence of God is more probable than not, as I have argued elsewhere that it is.) In this chapter I shall spell out the nature of the claim that there is God. Then, in the remaining chapters of Part I, I shall set out the central theological doctrines of Christianity (that is, doctrines about the nature and actions of God), and give a priori reasons for believing them to be true. By 'a priori reasons' I mean reasons arising from the very nature of God and from the general condition of the human race why we should expect them to be true. Then, in Part II, I shall argue that, given the moderate probability on other evidence that there is a God and given these a priori reasons, the historical evidence about the life and Resurrection of Jesus and the subsequent teaching of the Church makes it very probable that these doctrines are true. This historical evidence provides what I shall call 'a posteriori' reasons.

The Nature of God

What I mean by my claim that there is a **God** is that there is (at least) one divine person, who is essentially omnipotent, omniscient, perfectly free, and eternal. I shall call this claim 'theism'; it is a claim which Christianity, Judaism, and Islam and many other religions share. I shall assume for the rest of this chapter that—as Judaism and Islam claim—there is only one divine person, and I will call him 'God'. For the next ten pages I shall spell out what it is for there to be a divine person. (I shall refer to God as 'he'; but of course, though personal, God is neither male nor female.) In Chapter 2 and thereafter I shall need to use the word 'God' in a somewhat wider sense, in order to take account of the Christian doctrine of the Trinity.

A **person** is a being who has (or, when fully developed, will have) powers (to perform intentional actions, that is, actions which he or she means to do), beliefs, and free will (to choose among alternative actions without being compelled by irrational forces to do one rather than the other); when the beliefs and actions include ones of some sophistication (such as using language). I shall assume throughout this book that humans do have free will and so are persons. Ordinary human persons exist for a limited period of time, dependent on physical causes (their bodies and especially their brains) for their capacities to exercise their powers, form beliefs, and make choices. God is supposed to be unlimited in all these respects, and not to depend on anything for his existence or capacities.

God is supposed to be unlimited in his power; that is, **God is omnipotent**, he can do any action. He can make a physical universe exist, or move the stars, or sustain or abolish the physical causes which sustain humans in existence. He cannot do a logically impossible action, that is, an action which cannot be described without contradiction; and so he cannot make me both exist and not exist at the same time. But since it makes no sense to suppose that I could both exist and not exist at the same time, a logically impossible action is not really an action at all—any more than an imaginary person is really a person.

God is supposed to be unlimited in his beliefs; that is, **God is omniscient**; he has all true beliefs about everything (about which it is logically possible to have true beliefs), and in him they constitute not just beliefs but infallible knowledge. We know some things, and have false beliefs about other things. God, however, knows infallibly how many stars there are, whether it snowed in New York State on 1 January exactly 2 million years ago, and what you are now thinking about. (I will come back shortly to the issue of whether there are true beliefs which it is not logically possible for God to have.)

We humans have bodies. A body is a physical object through which we can make a difference to the world and learn about the world; and ordinary humans are tied down to acting and acquiring information through their bodies. I can only make a difference to the world by doing something with some part of my body—by using my arm to move something, or my mouth to tell you something. And I can only learn about the world by stimuli landing on my sense organs (light rays landing on my eyes or sound waves landing on my ears, for example). God, being omnipotent and omniscient, is not tied down to acting on and learning about the world through one particular physical object, and so **God does not need a body**.

God is supposed to be a **perfectly free person** in the sense of one whose choices are in no way limited by, that is, influenced by, irrational forces. He only desires to do an action in so far as he sees a reason for doing it, that is, in so far as he believes that it is a good action to do. Paradoxically, any being who is perfectly free (in this sense) will inevitably do in any situation that action which he believes to be the best possible action to do, if there is such an action. The **best action** is that which there is most reason to do. Although we humans are not in general perfectly free, we are sometimes in this situation where we are not influenced by irrational forces. Suppose you have plenty of money and you meet someone who needs some special medicine to keep him alive which he is too poor to buy, then (unless there is some special reason why this would be a bad thing to do) the best action would be to buy the medicine for him. If you believe that this would be the best action, and are not influenced by irrational forces, you will buy the medicine.

Sometimes, however, a perfectly free being will have a choice between two or more possible actions, only one of which he can do, when he believes that none of these actions are better than the other actions. There is, he believes, no best action but there are two or more **equal best** actions. Then he must simply choose which action to do—for no reason at all. We humans are also sometimes in this situation where we are not influenced by irrational forces and have a choice between two or more equal best actions. Suppose that you have only a little money and you meet two people A and B, who both need the special medicine, and you have only enough money to buy medicine to keep one alive. Then although you should give the money to one of those in need, it might be an equal best action to give it to A, and an equal best action to give it to B. There may be no reason for doing one of these actions rather than the other. If you believe this and are not influenced by irrational forces, you will do one of these actions, but which you will do depends on your free choice.

However, unlike a perfectly free person, humans are sometimes influenced by irrational forces. In so far as someone believes that an action is good, they will have a desire to do it. Such desires are **rational desires**; they are in accord with reason. And in so far as someone believes that an action is bad, they will have a desire not to do it. But **humans are sometimes subject to irrational desires**, that is, desires to do bad actions, or desires to do actions less good than a best action, which are stronger than the desire to do the best action. (By one desire being stronger than another one, I mean that the person concerned feels more inclined to yield to it.) A perfectly free being is not subject to irrational desires. Humans, however, are sometimes subject to bad desires, or desires to do a less good action, stronger than any desire to do a best action. But since (given my assumption that humans have free will) irrational desires only influence us and do not compel us, we are free to make the better choice, although it requires an effort of will to do so.

A smoker can choose whether to smoke a cigarette or not. The smoker has reasons for smoking (he likes it) and reasons for not smoking (it will make him more prone to lung cancer). And he may conclude that the reasons for not smoking are better than the reasons for smoking; indeed, that it would be bad to smoke. And yet the smoker may have an irrational desire to smoke, a desire which is stronger than his desire not to smoke (in that he feels more inclined to yield to it); and then he has the choice of whether or not to yield to the desire to smoke.

So, given that humans have free will, there are two aspects to this free will. When we are uninfluenced by irrational desires, we sometimes have a free choice between (what we believe to be) two or more equal best actions. When we are influenced by irrational desires to do an action which is (we believe) bad or less good than a best or equal best action, we can choose whether to do the better action or to yield to the irrational desire.

It is because it is up to us what to do in these two kinds of circumstance that, if anyone had a belief beforehand about what we would do, we would be able to make that belief false. Suppose that I have a choice between mowing the lawn and watching the television; I believe that it would be the best action to mow the lawn but I am subject to a stronger irrational desire to watch the television. What I will do depends on my free choice at that time. If you believe beforehand that I will watch the television, I have it in my power (by mowing the lawn) to bring it about that your belief proved false. Certainly if you know that my desire to watch the television is a strong one, you may rightly think it probable that I will watch the television, but you cannot be certain. It seems to follow that not even God can have an infallible true belief and so infallible knowledge about whether I will watch the television or mow the lawn. Generally **it looks as if it is not logically possible for God to know infallibly beforehand what a free agent will do** in such circumstances. But since God is omnipotent, it is only because he permits this that we have free will and are sometimes situated in circumstances where we are subject to irrational desires or have a choice between what we believe to be equal best actions. God is himself responsible for there being limits to his knowledge of how we will act; and he can take away our free will and so these limits to his knowledge of the future, whenever he chooses.

God himself, however, is supposed to be perfectly free and so not to be subject to irrational desires. So when there is an action which he believes to in the best available action, inevitably he will do it. Find since, being omniscients, he knows which actions are good and which are better than others, he will inevitably do the best action. He must, however, often have a choice between actions which he believes to be equal best; and for him this choice is simply the choice of which of equal best actions to do. It would seem to be an equal best action for God to arrange the initial state of the universe so that it eventually caused Uranus to rotate in a direction different from that of the other planets, as to arrange that state so that Uranus rotates in the same direction as the other planets. God cannot do both actions. It might have been an equal best action to choose Mary to be the mother of Jesus as to choose any of a number of possible mothers, but Jesus could have only one mother. And so on. But, since God is omnipotent, the range of incompatible equal best actions available to him is so much greater than the range available to us.

Further, God must often be in a situation where we cannot be, of having a choice between an infinite number of possible actions such that each action is, he believes, less good than some other action he could do. And since God knows which actions are good and which are better than others, this means a choice between an infinite number of actions, each of which is less good than some other action he could do. For example, animals which do not eat other animals are a good thing; they can be happy and loving. So the more of them the better (given that they are spread out among an infinite number of planets, so that they do not crowd each other out). So however many such animals God creates, it would have been better if he had created more. (And he could still have created more, even if he created an infinite number of them.) So although not influenced by irrational forces, **God cannot always do the best action**. He cannot do this when two or more possible actions are equal best; or where—as in the example just given—there is no best or equal best possible action; and he has then to exercise his choice between the actions in an arbitrary way.

It may be, however, that when there is no best action available to God, there may be a **best kind of action** available to God, such that it would be better to do some action of that kind than to do any number of actions of any other incompatible kind. For example, God can create creatures of many different types, including angels, humans, and animals. If it were the case that it would be better to create at least some humans (even if he creates no angels or animals) than to create any number of angels and animals and no humans, or to do an act of any other incompatible kind, then it would be a best kind of action for God to create some humans, although there would be no best number for him to create. If God believed that this is the case, then, I suggest, God, being influenced by reason alone, will inevitably create some humans. And if he believes that there are two or more **equal best kinds of action** available to him he will inevitably do some action of one of these kinds. So God will inevitably always do the best or equal best action, or an action of a best or equal best kind, where there is such an action. But he cannot always do the best action because there will not always be a best action.

Good actions can be divided into those that are **obligatory** (or **duties**), and those that go beyond obligation and which we call **supererogatory**. I am obliged (it is my duty) to pay my debts, but not to give my life to save that of a comrade—supremely, 'supererogatorily' good though it is that I should do so. To fail to fulfil an obligation is to do something **wrong**. A person is in some way at fault for doing what is wrong, and if he believes that he is doing wrong, he is blameworthy for doing it; but he does not deserve praise merely for fulfilling his obligations (doing his duty). And he is in some way meritorious for doing what is supererogatory; and if he believes that he is doing something supererogatory, he is praiseworthy for doing it. Positive obligations normally arise because of benefits received (I owe my parents much because they have done much for me) or because of commitments, explicit or implicit. I must keep my promises and pay my debts because I have explicitly committed myself to doing so. And I must feed my children because by bringing them into existence I have implicitly committed myself to doing so. Negative obligations—obligations not to do things—normally concern not damaging other people. It is wrong to steal or kill (possibly subject to some qualifications). Obligations are a limited set of good actions, and most of us can fulfil all our obligations, although sometimes we find ourselves with incompatible obligations. Although God cannot always do the best, he can always fulfil all his obligations. As the source of the existence of all other beings, he does not owe anyone anything as a result of benefits received or for any other reason; and since there is good reason to ensure this, he will ensure that he never enters into commitments which he could not fulfil. For example, he will never promise to one person that he will do some action and also to another person that he will not do that action. And since it is always a best action to fulfil an obligation when one has no conflicting obligations, **God will fulfil all his obligations**. Paradoxically, then, God, being perfectly free and omniscient, can do no bad action and above all (within the class of bad actions) no wrong action.

It follows from the argument of the last few pages that we must understand God being **perfectly good** as God doing no bad actions and many good actions, and always doing the best action or an equal best action (or action of a best or equal best kind) where there is one available to him.

God is also a **source of moral obligation** in that his command to us to do some action makes it obligatory for us to do that action when it would not otherwise be obligatory. Many truths of morality hold whether or not there is a God. Clearly it is good to feed the starving and obligatory to keep promises (possibly subject to certain exceptions), whether or not there is a God. But among truths of morality which hold independently of God is the truth that we have an obligation to please our benefactors (those who are the source of much good to us)—within limits. It is because of this that children have a (limited) obligation to please their parents (those who are not merely biological parents but nurturing parents who feed, clothe, educate, and care for them in many other ways). And an obvious way to please benefactors is to obey their commands. But if there is a God, he is so much more the source of good things to us than are our parents. He keeps us in being from moment to moment, and all the good things which our parents and others provide for us they can provide only because God allows them to do so. So if God commands us to do some action, it will be our duty to do it. Maybe there are limits on what God has the right to command; having created humans as free rational creatures, perhaps he does not have the right to tell them what to do every minute of their lives. But, if so, being perfectly good, he will not command anyone to do what he has no right to command. For to command what you have no right to command is wrong.

God is **eternal**. But this has been understood in two different senses: either as the claim that God is timeless (he does not exist in time, or at any rate in our time) or as the claim that God is everlasting (he existed at every moment of past time, exists now, and will exist at every moment of future time). In my opinion the timeless view is incompatible with everything else that religious believers have wanted to say about God. For example, it does seem strongly that God being omniscient entails that he hears the prayers of humans at the same time as they utter them; yet on the timeless view God does not exist at the same time as (simultaneously with) any moment on our timescale. For this and other reasons I shall in future understand God being eternal as God being **everlasting**; though it might be possible to re-express much of the rest of what I have to say on the assumption that God is timeless rather than everlasting. Being everlasting, God is unlimited in the time during which he exists.

Because God is omnipotent, and omniscient, everything else that exists exists only because he knowingly causes or allows someone else to cause it to exist. Hence he could have prevented the universe from ever existing and he could annihilate it at any moment. So its existence from moment to moment depends entirely on him; in that sense **God is creator and sustainer of the universe** and of all that it contains. The universe may or may not have always existed—we do not know whether the universe had a beginning. But if it had a beginning, God brought it into existence then; and if it has always existed, God has always kept it in existence.

Being omnipotent, omniscient, etc. are properties of God. God, like individual persons, stones, tables, and planets, is a thing; philosophers sometimes call these things 'substances'. **Substances** have **properties**: a certain table may have the properties of being brown, square, and weighing 5 kg. Some of the properties of substances are essential to them. A property is an essential property of a substance if that substance could not lose that property without ceasing to exist. Being brown is not an essential property of my table: the table could continue to exist if it were repainted red. But occupying space is an essential property of the table: if it ceased to occupy space, it would cease to exist. The properties of substances include both their monadic properties (properties which they have in themselves apart from their relations to other substances) and their relational properties (their relations to other things). Being brown, square, and weighing 5 kg are monadic properties; whereas 'being 10 ft away from a wall' or 'being made by a carpenter' or 'being an elder brother' are relational properties.

God is supposed not merely to be omnipotent, omniscient, perfectly free, and eternal, but to be so essentially—if God ceased to be omnipotent, omniscient, or perfectly free, he would cease to exist; and (since being eternal is also an essential property of God) a being who could cease to exist could never have been God at all. God cannot commit suicide. **These properties are essential to God.** They belong to God's nature or essence. But **God has other properties which are non-essential** (accidental or contingent); he has these accidental properties because he chooses to have them. Among these properties is being creator and sustainer of the universe: the universe exists only because he chooses that it should exist. The exact degree of our power, knowledge, and freedom are, of course, not properties which make ordinary human persons the particular people we are (although we need to have, at least when fully developed, some degree or other of these properties). I remain the same person if I forget many things or lose the power to move my legs.

Ordinary human persons could be duplicated in that there could be a different person with exactly the same properties, monadic and relational, as I have. There could be in another world exactly like this world in all other respects another person exactly like me in his appearance, mental life, and history, and writing a book entitled *Was Jesus God?* Or, instead of me, my parents could have produced a different son with exactly the same genes, who went on to have the experiences and live the life which I have lived—without me ever having existed. You can see this by imagining yourself being shown before your birth a film of what will happen in a future world (and which would picture in some way all the experiences and thoughts which the inhabitants of different bodies would have). You would still want to know whether you would live in that world and which body and which experiences and thoughts you would have. Philosophers sometimes express this point by saying that each human being has (as well as some properties essential for all humans) a **thisness**, which is not a property or combination of properties but something underlying those properties which makes him or her the particular human they are. Although ordinary humans have thisness, not all things have thisness. Gravitational fields, for example, do not have thisness; any gravitational field which had the same strength, shape, and size as the one which surrounds our earth would be that gravitational field. And it is a controversial issue whether fundamental particles, such as electrons and protons, have thisness; and so, for example, whether the world would be any different if you exchanged the positions of two electrons.

Does God have thisness? Fairly few philosophers and theologians have faced this question, but those who have claim in effect that God does not have thisness. For example, Augustine (the great theologian who was a bishop in North Africa in the fourth century AD) denied that God is properly called a 'substance' that 'has' properties. God, Augustine claimed, is more properly called an 'essence' because he 'is' his properties. That is, the essential properties of God which I have listed (and perhaps deeper properties from which these derive) are what makes God God. This means that things couldn't be different in the respect that a different God (with all the same properties as the actual God) was in charge of the universe. For any being who had all the same properties as the actual God would be the actual God. For reasons of a kind which I shall give later in this chapter, I think that Augustine's view is correct: if there is a God, **God does not have thisness**. If so, then it will be an aspect of the divine nature that he has no thisness; it will not be a contingent feature of God. We shall see in Chapter 2 that, if God has thisness, there are important consequences for the doctrine of the Trinity.

As well as having the properties which I have analysed so far, God is supposed to be in some sense a 'necessary being', but, like 'eternal', this has been understood in different senses. Some philosophers hold that God is a logically necessary being in that 'There is no God' involves a contradiction. That seems to me manifestly false. 'There is no God' makes a coherent claim (does not involve a self-contradiction) which we can understand, even if we believe it to be false. But all theists wish to maintain that **God is** an **ontologically necessary** being in that his existence is not contingent on anything else: no other individual or physical or metaphysical principle causes (or has any share in causing) the existence of God. But how this is to be understood depends on whether there is more than one divine person, and so I shall postpone discussion of this issue until Chapter 2.

Reasons to Believe That There Is a God

Different people have different reasons for believing that there is a God. Some people have deep private 'religious' experiences, as it seems to them, of the presence of God. Others believe that there is a God on the basis of testimony; that is, because their parents or teachers or priest tell them that there is a God, and they think their parents or whoever are knowledgeable and trustworthy. It seems to me that **religious experience** provides a good reason for believing—so long as that experience is overwhelming, and you don't know of any strong objections to the existence of God. If we didn't believe that what it seems to us obvious that we are experiencing (perceiving or feeling) is really there, when there are no good reasons for doubting that that thing is really there, we couldn't believe anything. And the **testimony** of others that there is a God also provides a good reason for believing—so long as everyone tells us the same thing, and we don't know of any strong reasons why they might be mistaken. If we didn't believe what others told us, for example, about history or geography, until we had checked it out for ourselves, we would have very few beliefs. But I think that very few people have overwhelming religious experiences, and in the modern world most people come into contact not merely with those who tell them that there is a God but also with those who tell them that there is no God, and most people are aware of strong objections to the existence of God.

So I think that most people in the modern world need to have their experiences or the testimony of others reinforced by reasons to suppose that the objections to the existence of God do not work. But instead or as well as such reasons, they also need a positive argument for the existence of God which starts from very obvious observable data if they are to have good reason to believe that there is a God. And for some people such an argument will provide the sole basis for their belief. Arguments of this kind are called **arguments of natural theology**. I believe that there is a good argument for the existence of God from the most general features of the universe. I have given this argument in other places, including in the short companion book *Is There a God?* All I can do here is to show what kind of argument it is.

Theism, the claim that there is a God, **is an explanatory hypothesis**, one which purports to explain why certain observed data (or evidence) are as they are. Many scientific or historical hypotheses are explanatory hypotheses: they purport to explain data which the scientist has observed in his laboratory or the historian has discovered in the course of an archaeological investigation. **Such a hypothesis is probably true in so far as it is a simple hypothesis which leads us to expect the data which are otherwise unexpected** (that is, make it probable that those data would occur, when otherwise it is not probable that they would occur), **and fits in with** 'background evidence' or '**prior evidence**'. Suppose that there has been a burglary: money has been stolen from a safe. The detective puts forward the hypothesis, to explain the money having been stolen, that John robbed the safe. If John did rob the safe, it would be quite probable that his fingerprints would be on the safe, that someone might report having seen him near the scene of the crime at the time it was committed, and that money of the amount stolen might be found in his house. These are data to be expected with some modest degree of probability if John robbed the safe, and much less to be expected if he did not rob the safe; they therefore constitute positive evidence, evidence favouring the hypothesis. On the other hand, if John robbed the safe, it would be most unexpected (it would be most improbable) that many people would report seeing him in a foreign country at the time of the burglary. Such reports would constitute negative evidence, evidence counting strongly against the hypothesis. I shall call evidence of either kind **posterior evidence**, the consequences to be expected or not to be expected if the hypothesis were true. In so far as a hypothesis makes it probable that we would find all the data we find, and in so far as it would be improbable that we would find these data if the hypothesis were false, that increases the probability of the hypothesis. The more probable it is that we'd find the data if the hypothesis were true, and the more improbable it is that we'd find the data if the hypothesis were false, the more probable the data make the hypothesis.

But a hypothesis is only rendered probable by data in so far as it is **simple**. Consider the following hypothesis as an explanation of the detective's positive data: David stole the money; quite unknown to David, George dressed up to look like John at the scene of the crime; Tony planted John's fingerprints on the safe just for fun; and, unknown to the others, Stephen hid money stolen from another robbery in John's garage. If this complicated hypothesis were true, we would expect to find all the positive data which I described, when it is not nearly as probable otherwise that we would find the data. But the data do not make the complicated hypothesis probable, although they do make the hypothesis that John robbed the safe probable; and that is because the latter hypothesis is simple. A hypothesis is simple in so far as it postulates few substances and simply describable properties, few kinds of substances and simply describable properties, including properties of behaving in simple ways. The detective's original hypothesis postulates only one substance (John) doing one thing (robbing the safe) which leads us to expect the data; while the rival hypothesis which I have just set out postulates many substances (many persons) doing different things.

But as well as the posterior evidence of the kind which I illustrated, there may be background evidence, or **prior evidence**: evidence which is not a (probable) consequence of the truth or falsity of the hypothesis in question, but comes from an area outside the scope of that hypothesis. We may have evidence about what John has done on other occasions, for example, that he has often robbed safes in the past. This latter evidence would make the hypothesis that John robbed the safe on this occasion much more probable than it would be without this evidence. Conversely, evidence that John has lived a crime-free life in the past would

make it much less probable that he robbed the safe on this occasion.
A hypothesis fits with such prior evidence in so far as the prior
evidence makes probable a theory (e.g. that John is a regular
safe-robber), which in turn makes the hypothesis in question more
probable than it would otherwise be.

The criteria for assessing the detective's hypothesis apply generally to assessing hypotheses proposed by scientists or historians.
If a scientist's data are such as he expects to find (that is, are such
as it is probable will occur) if his hypothesis is true, that makes the
hypothesis more probable than it would be otherwise. If they are
such as he expects not to find (that is, are such as it is probable will
not occur) if the hypothesis is true, that makes the hypothesis less
probable than it would be otherwise. The simpler the hypothesis,
the more probable it is; and a very simple hypothesis is a lot
more probable than any other hypothesis. And if the hypothesis is
concerned only with a narrow field (e.g. the behaviour of a single
planet), it has to fit with what we know about the wider physical
world (e.g. how other planets behave). For many hypotheses there
may be no relevant prior evidence, and the greater the scope of a
hypothesis (that is, the more it purports to tell us about the world),
the less prior evidence there will be. For a very large-scale theory
of physics (such as quantum theory) there will be few physical
phenomena apart from those within its scope (which it purports to
explain), and so little, if any, prior evidence.

The data (the **posterior evidence for theism**) to which arguments of natural theology typically appeal include the most general
features of the universe: that every particle of matter behaves in
exactly the same lawlike way as every other particle (obeys the
same 'laws of nature', for example, Newton's law of gravity); that
the initial state of the universe (the Big Bang) and the laws of nature
are such as to bring about the eventual existence (some 13 billion
years later) of human beings; and that these humans are conscious
beings (have a mental life of thought, feeling, and choice). In *Is There
a God?* and elsewhere I argue that, in virtue of God's omnipotence
and perfect goodness, it is quite probable that these data would
occur if there were a God (because he would bring them about);
and very improbable that they would occur if there were no God.

The way in which I have spelled out the hypothesis of theism
earlier in this chapter has the consequence that **theism is a very
simple hypothesis**. It postulates the existence of one entity (one

god, not many gods), with very few very simply describable properties. A person with no limits to his power, knowledge, freedom,
and life is the simplest kind of person there could be. Infinite
power is power with zero limits. Infinite knowledge is knowledge
with zero limits because it involves no limit (except one imposed
by logic) to the number of well-justified true beliefs. Perfect
freedom means that the person's choices are unlimited by irrational
desires. Eternity means no temporal limit to life. And God being
ontologically necessary, meaning that there are no others on whom
he depends, obviously fits well with his other properties. It is also
simpler to suppose that God has these properties essentially, for
that makes God a more unified being; it means that the divine
properties not merely do not, but could not, come apart. And it is
simpler to suppose that God is what he is solely in virtue of his
essential properties; that is, he has **no underlying 'thisness'**—for
that is a more economical supposition. It means that it is not an
extra truth about how things are that this God rather than that
God is in charge of the universe. If God does not have thisness,
any God in charge of the universe would be the same God as any
God in charge of the universe. God being what he is in virtue of
the essential properties which I have listed makes God not quite a
person in the sense in which we are 'persons'.

Theism is such a wide-ranging hypothesis (it purports to explain
all the most general features of the universe) that there is **no prior
evidence**; all the evidence (whether positive or negative) is within
its scope—posterior evidence. So if I am right that theism is a very
simple hypothesis, which makes it quite probable that there would
be a universe with the most general features which I have described
when this would be very improbable otherwise, there is a good
argument from this posterior evidence to the probable existence of
God. In arguing in this way, I have sought to articulate a rigorous
argument of a kind which many philosophers, Christians, Jews,
Muslims, and others have been giving for the past two or three
thousand years.

Theodicy

Not merely do most people need positive arguments in favour of
the existence of God if they are to have good reason to believe

that there is a God, but they also need grounds to believe that arguments against the existence of God do not work. And that in particular means grounds to believe that arguments against the existence of God from the fact that there is much pain and other suffering in the world do not work. Like many other philosophers, I have attempted to produce a 'theodicy' (an explanation of why a good God would allow suffering), among other places in *Is There a God?* It attempts to show that it is not improbable that, if there were a God, such suffering would occur.

The basic structure of my theodicy, which is relevant to subsequent chapters of the present book, is as follows. A good God who creates humans does not merely want to make us happy (in the sense of doing what we want to be doing). He wants us to be good people and to be happy in being good people, and he also wants us to become good people by our own choices. **God wants to give us deep responsibility for ourselves and each other.** And he wants us to choose to exercise our responsibility in the right way. So he takes a big risk with us. He gives us free will and power to make a difference to our own future and to the future of each other, and leaves it up to us how we choose to exercise our power. Our choices, as I noted earlier, are influenced by our desires, but, given that we have free will, they are not fully determined by them. We can only have deep responsibility for ourselves if we have the power to ruin our lives (for example, by taking heroin), or alternatively to live greatly worthwhile lives. We can only have responsibility for others if it really is up to us whether things go well or badly with those others; so we must have the power to hurt them or neglect them, as well as the power to benefit them. And if we are to have great responsibility, God must allow us to hurt each other a lot. Humans are so made that each time we make a good choice, it becomes easier to make a good choice next time; and each time we make a bad choice, it becomes easier to make a bad choice next time. If I tell the truth today when it is difficult, it will be easier to do so again tomorrow. But if I lie today, it will be harder to avoid lying tomorrow. So gradually over time we change the desires which influence us, and **we may eventually form either a very good character or a very bad character**.

However, if the only suffering in the world were that caused by humans (or allowed to occur through human negligence), many of us would not have very much opportunity to make those crucial choices which are so important for forming our characters. **Humans need the pain and disability** caused by disease and old age if we are to have the opportunity to choose freely whether to be patient and cheerful, or to be gloomy and resentful, in the face of our own suffering; and the opportunity to choose freely to show or not to show compassion to others who suffer, and to give or not to give our time and money to helping them. God cannot do the logically impossible: he cannot give us the freedom to hurt each other and at the same time ensure that we won't. Hence if God is to give us the great goods that I have described, he must provide us with bad desires and pain and other suffering in significant strength—at least for the short period of our earthly lives. I am not claiming that he must provide these bad things, only that he must provide them if he is also to give us the great good things. I am inclined to think that it would be an **equal best action for God to create humans** with the great goods which I have described together with the bad things which must accompany them, **and an equal best action for God not to create humans** with either the good things or the bad things.

As our creator and benefactor who provides for us lives full of so many good things, **God has the right to impose on some of us bad things**—not just bad desires, but suffering—and to allow us to be hurt by others, if this is necessary for our own well-being or the well-being of others. Parents have a very limited right to allow their children to suffer for the sake of some good to others. They have the right to send a daughter to a neighbourhood school which she will not enjoy very much, in order to cement community relations. And they have the right to entrust a younger son to the care of an elder son, even if there is a risk that the elder son will hurt the younger son to some degree, in order that the elder son may have the responsibility for his younger brother. It is nevertheless **a great privilege to be of use to someone else**, not just by what you choose to do but by what you are allowed to suffer. The girl sent to the neighbouring school is privileged to be allowed to contribute to cementing community relations by her less than enjoyable schooling. The rights of parents over children are, however, very limited because it is only to a very limited extent that they are the source of the existence and well-being of their children. God, who keeps humans in existence from moment to moment and gives them all their limited powers and freedom, has a far greater right to impose suffering on humans for some good purpose. But in my view God's right to impose suffering is also limited: he must provide lives for us in which there is more good than bad. When we take into account the great benefit of life itself and the great benefit to any sufferer of the privilege of being of use to others, there will be few earthly lives in which the bad exceeds the good (except in those cases where a person chooses to live a life of this kind). But if there are any humans in whose lives (not as a consequence of their own choices) the bad exceeds the good, God has an obligation to give to those humans at least a limited life after death in which the good exceeds the bad; and in his omnipotence he can and must do this.

Such is the very broad outline of my theodicy. A theodicy is a necessary part of a natural theology, which most of us need if we are to have a good reason to believe that there is a God.

Christian Doctrines

Christianity makes certain further claims about God, what he is like and what he has done and will do, beyond those described in the opening section of this chapter. The purpose of this book is to discuss these further claims, the doctrines which distinguish Christianity from other religions. Most of these doctrines concern Jesus, a Jew who was born around the first year of the Christian era (AD I), lived and taught in what is now Israel and its surrounding territories, and died in about AD 30, crucified by the occupying Roman army at the instigation of the Jewish authorities. (Since Christians regarded him as the 'Messiah', the new king whom God had promised for Israel, they called him 'the Christ', meaning 'the anointed king'.) Some of these doctrines are fairly easy-to-understand historical claims: for example, the Resurrection of Jesus (that he rose from the dead in his human body three days after his Crucifixion). Other doctrines are sophisticated metaphysical doctrines: for example, the doctrine of the Trinity, that there are three divine 'persons', 'the Father', 'the Son', and 'the Holy Spirit', who together form one God; and the doctrine of the Incarnation, that Jesus was 'the Son', the second person of the Trinity who (while remaining divine) became human in Jesus. And Christian doctrines also include certain moral doctrines, that is, specifically

Christian views about which actions are good or bad, obligatory or wrong.

I claimed earlier that an explanatory hypothesis is probably true in so far as it is a simple hypothesis which fits in with 'prior evidence' and leads us to expect data which are not otherwise to be expected. I pointed out that, when we are considering theism, the hypothesis that there is a divine person, and our data are the most general phenomena we can observe, there will be no prior evidence. But we come now to the more detailed hypothesis of Christian theism (the specifically Christian doctrines about God). We will already have a view about how probable is theism by itself ('bare theism') on the evidence described earlier (our own religious experience, the testimony of others, and the very general features of the universe, and also the data of pain and other suffering). All this evidence taken together gives a certain degree of probability to the existence of God (that is, that there is a divine person of the kind described earlier); and the more probable it makes the existence of God, the more probable it makes Christian theism. For clearly Christian theism can be true only if bare theism is true; but since Christian theism makes further claims beyond those of bare theism, this earlier evidence will not make Christian theism as probable as it makes bare theism.

The earlier evidence which formed the posterior evidence for bare theism forms the **prior evidence for Christian theism**. The reader must consider (in the light of arguments to be found in *Is There a God?* or elsewhere) how probable or improbable that evidence makes the hypothesis of bare theism (as I have expounded it). The more probable it makes bare theism, and the more probable bare theism makes Christian theism (that is, the more probable it is that, if there is a God, the specially Christian doctrines about him are true), the more probable it makes Christian theism. To the extent to which this holds I shall say that Christian theism 'fits in' with the prior evidence. That prior evidence therefore gives a certain **prior probability** to Christian theism (it provides a priori reasons for believing it to be true); and the better Christian theism fits in with that evidence, the greater is that prior probability.

I contrast this prior evidence with the **posterior evidence for Christian theism**, which is the historical evidence about Jesus and the subsequent Christian Church. (This provides a posteriori reasons for believing Christian theism to be true.) In so far as the historical evidence is to be expected if Christian theism is true and not otherwise (that is, in so far as Christian theism makes it probable that this historical evidence will occur, when it would not be probable otherwise), that will raise the probability of Christian theism well above its prior probability, and give it what is called its **posterior probability**, its probability on the total available evidence.

The prior evidence for Christian theism will make it probable (to some degree, large or small) that there is a God of the kind which I have analysed earlier, in particular an omnipotent and perfectly good God. And **God's perfect goodness makes it probable that he will do certain things** rather than other things. For we have some understanding of what a good person will do. Good people try to make other people happy, happy in doing and enjoying worthwhile things (but not happy in causing pain to others). Good people try to help other people for whom they are responsible (for example, their own children) to be good people themselves. Good people seek to share what they have with others and to cooperate with others in all these activities. Good people forgive those who make reparation and ask for forgiveness. But also, as I claimed earlier, good people may sometimes to a limited extent and for a limited period allow those for whom they are responsible to suffer and to cause others to suffer if only by so doing can some good purpose be achieved.

We derive this understanding of what it is to be a good person by reflecting on what a good ordinary human person will do. But a divine person of course, although personal, is different from ordinary human persons. And so we must reflect what difference it would make to how a good person would act if there were no limits to his power, knowledge, etc., and if he were the source of the existence from moment to moment of all other things. I shall be suggesting in subsequent chapters that this prior understanding of what God is likely to do in virtue of the sort of being he is gives us some prior reason for supposing the various Christian doctrines to be true. What they tell us (for example, that God became human, or provided atonement for our wrongdoing) is, I shall be arguing, the sort of thing that it is probable that a God would do—just as, if John is a habitual criminal, that makes it probable that he will commit another crime. But such reflection can only give us *some* idea of what God is likely to do. There are many different equally good actions which a good God might do, some of them incompatible with each other. It might be equally good, for example, for God to let us try to discover for ourselves some moral truths (for example, whether abortion and euthanasia are always wrong or sometimes permissible), or to tell us all the answers to disputed moral questions. It is good for God to let us try to discover these things for ourselves; but it is also good for us to know the answers in order to help us to avoid doing what is wrong, and if we haven't had total success in discovering all the answers for ourselves, it might be equally good for God to reveal the answers to us, as to let us go on trying to discover them. And even if moral reflection tells us that God would be quite likely to do a certain action (for example, to reveal moral truths to us), it cannot tell us when and where he will do this. Analogously, mere reflection on the fact that John is a habitual criminal will show that he is likely to commit another crime, but it cannot tell us when and where he will do this. In both cases we need posterior evidence.

In the case of divine action, the **posterior evidence is historical evidence** that such and such an event has occurred in human history which it is to some extent probable that God would bring about and would have been unlikely to occur unless God had brought it about; for example, evidence that some prophet rose from the dead. I shall be arguing that God has reason to reveal certain truths to us via a prophet, and that to show that what the prophet teaches is indeed a revelation from God he needs to associate that teaching with a great miracle, a violation of laws of nature which God alone can bring about. So if we have evidence that some prophet who taught what (in virtue of its content) looks like a revelation from God, and was killed for that teaching, subsequently rose from the dead, that is—I shall be arguing—posterior evidence that what the prophet taught is true. The posterior evidence is evidence of the occurrence of an event which the prior evidence gives us some reason to expect, but about which we need posterior evidence to make it overall probable that it occurred and to inform us where and when it occurred. The stronger the prior evidence (that is, the more probable it makes the existence of God), the weaker the posterior (historical) evidence may be while still making it overall probable that Christian doctrines are true. And even if the prior evidence (e.g. from natural theology) for the existence of God is not very strong, still if the posterior evidence for Christian doctrines is strong, it may yet make those doctrines overall probable, and thereby, of course, make theism itself probable.

While different kinds of Christians (Roman Catholic, Orthodox, monophysite, 'Nestorian', Anglican, and Protestant) have slightly different beliefs from each other, I shall be concerned only with the **central doctrines of Christianity, common to virtually all Christians** from very early in the Christian era. These consist, as I noted earlier, of historical, metaphysical, and moral doctrines. I shall group together the central doctrines of the two former kinds and call them 'theological doctrines' (doctrines about the nature of God and his actions in the world). These were all formulated in what was for a thousand years the common creed of virtually all Christians, **the Nicene Creed**, given its final form by the Council of Constantinople in AD 381. (It is called the 'Nicene Creed' because the Council of Constantinople claimed that this creed put into words the main claims of the Council of Nicaea held in AD 325. The group of those who rejected this creed (called 'Arians') very soon became a small minority, and then virtually ceased to exist.) The Creed (translated from the original Greek) is as follows:

I believe in one God, Father almighty, maker of Heaven and earth, and of all things visible and invisible. And in one Lord, Jesus Christ, the only-begotten Son of God, begotten from the Father before all ages, Light from Light, true God from true God, begotten not made, of the same essence as the Father; through him all things were made. For us humans and for our salvation he came down from the heavens, and was incarnate from the Holy Spirit and the Virgin Mary and became human. He was crucified also for us under Pontius Pilate, and suffered and was buried; he rose again on the third day, in accordance with the Scriptures, and ascended into the heavens, and is seated at the right hand of the Father. He will come again in glory to judge the living and the dead, and his kingdom will have no end. And in the Holy Spirit, the Lord, the Giver of life, who proceeds from the Father, who together with Father and Son is worshipped and together glorified; who spoke through the Prophets. In one Holy, Catholic and Apostolic Church. I confess one Baptism for the forgiveness of sins. I await the resurrection of the dead and the life of the age to come.

In the next five chapters of Part I, I shall elucidate these theological doctrines; and also lay out the a priori reasons for believing them to be true. That is, I shall consider how far it is made probable by the nature of God as described so far (and by very general facts about the human race and its history) that God would have the further nature and act in human history through some human person and community in the way that these doctrines claim that he acted through Jesus and his church. Then, in Part II, I shall analyse the posterior evidence, the relevant historical evidence which we need in order to show that these doctrines are true of Jesus and the Christian Church—in particular that Jesus was not merely a human person but God living among us. So I shall be discussing each of the doctrines contained in the Creed both in Part I (to consider the a priori reasons for believing them) and in Part II (to discuss the a posteriori reasons.) I have entitled Part I 'God Loves Us' because I shall argue that God would have shown his love for humans by acting in human history in the way described. I have entitled Part II 'God Shows Us That He loves Us' because I shall be arguing that (given the prior evidence) the posterior (historical) evidence shows that God has acted in this way. But before coming to the issue of how we may expect God to act towards us, I argue that we may expect God to have a certain nature beyond that which I have described so far, a nature asserted by the Creed in the doctrine of the Trinity.

2 GOD IS LOVE

God Is a Trinity

The reasons which people have for believing there to be a God which I described in Chapter 1 are, I claimed there, reasons for believing that there is (at least) one divine person; that is, a person who is essentially omnipotent, omniscient, perfectly free, and eternal. I called that person in Chapter 1 'God'; but the use of that word (with a capital 'G') suggests that there is only one such person. In this chapter I wish to explore the issue of whether there is more than one divine person. So in this chapter and subsequently—following a tradition which I will explain in due course—I will call that divine person, in whose existence we have reasons from religious experience, or testimony, or natural theology to believe, '**God the Father**'. In effect Judaism and Islam believe only in God the Father. But Christianity claims that there are three divine persons who depend totally on each other and act together as one 'personal being', a Trinity. (Distinguish this from 'tritheism', which is the belief that there are three independent gods.) I will now set out a priori reasons for believing this to be true; that is, reasons why, given that God the Father exists, we would expect there to be a Trinity; and then show how this belief was expressed in the Nicene Creed.

Suppose the Father existed alone. For a person to exist alone, when he could cause others to exist and interact with him, would be bad. A divine person is a perfectly good person, and that involves being a loving person. A loving person needs someone to love; and **perfect love is love of an equal**, totally mutual love, which is what is involved in a perfect marriage. While, of course, the love of a parent for a child is of immense value, it is not the love of equals; and what makes it as valuable as it is, is that the parent is seeking to make the child (as she grows up) into an equal. A perfectly good solitary person would seek to bring about another such person, with whom to share all that she has. There is an ancient principle called the Dionysian principle, which states that goodness is diffusive: it spreads itself. The Father will bring into existence another divine person with whom to share his rule of the universe. Following tradition, let us call that other person '**God the Son**'.

But if the Father only began to cause the existence of the Son at some moment of time, say a trillion trillion years ago, that would be too late: for all eternity before that time he would not have manifested his perfect goodness. At each moment of everlasting time **the Father must always cause the Son to exist**, and so always keep the Son in being. Augustine wrote (*On Diverse Questions* 83 q.50) that if the Father 'wished to "beget" the Son [that is, cause the Son to exist], and was unable to do it, he would have been weak; if he was able to do it but did not wish to, he would have failed to do it because of "envy"' (that is, because he wished to be the only divine person). A solitary God would have been an ungenerous god and so no God. Although the Father is the (eternal) cause of the Son's existence, and the Son is not the cause of the Father's existence, they will in a certain sense be mutually dependent on each other. For the Father always to cause the Son to exist would be a unique best act of the Father; and so, since being perfectly good is an essential property of a divine person, the Father will inevitably always cause the Son to exist. Hence the Father would not exist at all unless he caused the Son to exist; and that is why he requires the Son to exist for his own existence. And the perfect goodness of Father and Son means that they love each other without limit.

A twosome can be selfish. A marriage in which husband and wife are interested only in each other and do not seek to spread the love they have for each other is a deficient marriage. (And of course the obvious way, but not the only way, in which they can spread their love is by having children.) **The love of the Father for the Son must include** a wish to cooperate with the Son in **further total sharing with an equal**; and hence the need for a third member of the Trinity, whom, following tradition, we may call **the Holy Spirit**, whom they will love and by whom they will be loved. A universe in which there was only sharing and not cooperation in further sharing would have been a deficient universe; it would have lacked a certain kind of goodness. The Father and the Son would have been less than perfectly good unless they sought to spread their mutual love of cooperating in further sharing with an equal.

In the twelfth century Richard of St Victor made this point and gave a further argument for it. He wrote (*On the Trinity* 3. 14 and 3. 15) that anyone who really loves someone will seek the good of that person by finding some third person for him to love and be loved by. This demand can of course only be satisfied by having no less than three divine persons. And, as with the bringing about of the Son, any moment of time at which the Father and Son brought about the Spirit for the first time would have been too late; they would not have been perfectly good if there was a period at which they existed alone without the Spirit. Hence **the Trinity must have always existed**. Although the Father and the Son caused the Spirit to exist, and not vice versa, all are (in a sense) mutually dependent for the same reason as before. This is that, since being perfectly good is an essential characteristic of a divine being, unless Father and Son caused the Holy Spirit to exist, they would not exist themselves. And the perfect goodness of Father, Son, and Spirit means that they love each other without limit. The essence of the divine society is love.

But how could there be more than one divine person? Clearly there could be three persons who are each essentially omniscient, perfectly free (and so perfectly good), and eternal. But how could all of them be essentially omnipotent as well? Even though they are each perfectly good, will not one try to do one equal best act while another tries to do an incompatible equal best act? Maybe the Father will try to make Uranus rotate in the same direction as the other planets while the Son tries to make Uranus rotate in a different direction (which looks like an equally good action). They cannot both succeed. The only way in which conflict can be avoided is if each of the three persons see themselves as having at any one time different spheres of activity, because it would be bad for them to act outside their sphere of activity. Then each could be omnipotent, but there would be no conflict because in virtue of their perfect goodness no divine person would try to do an act of a kind which would be incompatible with an act which another divine person was trying to do. Each would be omnipotent in that, for example, if he chose to make Uranus rotate in a clockwise direction, he would succeed; but only one would choose to do so. The Father brings about, sustains, and eliminates things in one sphere of activity, the Son does this in another sphere, and the Spirit does this in a third sphere.

But what could determine which divine person had which sphere of activity? Persons caused to exist by another person have obligations to the person who caused them. So **the Father**, being perfectly good, will seek to avoid any conflict by **laying down for each divine person his sphere of activity**; and the others, being perfectly good, will recognize an obligation to conform to his rule. So there will be no possibility of conflict.

If divine persons other than the Father did not derive their existence from the Father, there would be no one with the authority to lay down the sphere of activity for each divine person. Then divine persons would be like two people approaching each other on a sidewalk from opposite directions who try to avoid bumping into each other. Both could try to do this by moving towards the edge of the sidewalk nearest the road; and then, seeing that the other was also doing this, move away towards the edge furthest from the road. Without some arbitrary rule (such as 'Always walk on the left') they would only avoid bumping into each other by luck; and an arbitrary rule requires a rule-giver. Hence **there could not be two or more independent divine persons**. So only the Father can be ontologically necessary (in the sense defined in Chapter 1, that is, he is not caused to exist by anything else). But since the perfect goodness of the Father requires the other two divine persons to exist just as inevitably as the Father exists, they are what I will call 'metaphysically necessary'. I define a being as 'metaphysically necessary' if either it is ontologically necessary or it is inevitably caused to exist by an ontologically necessary being. Their equal inevitable existence makes the members of the Trinity equally worthy of worship. **All three members of the Trinity are metaphysically necessary persons, but the Father alone is ontologically necessary.** And the whole Trinity is ontologically necessary because nothing else caused it to exist.

I claimed in Chapter 1 that the simplest and so by far the most probable kind of God would lack thisness; and what I called 'God' in Chapter 1 is what I am calling 'God the Father' in this chapter. Something lacks thisness, the reader will recall, if it is what it is solely in virtue of its properties and not in virtue of something underlying its properties. Put in another way, if something has thisness, it could have a duplicate—something which has all the same properties but is not that thing. We humans have thisness, because instead of me there could have been a different person exactly like me who had the same body and all the same thoughts and feelings and yet was not me. Now if God the Father lacks thisness, he is what he is in virtue of his properties. These include the divine properties which the Son and Spirit also have. If **the Son and Spirit** are to be beings of the same kind as the Father, they must **also lack thisness**. So what makes each of them the particular divine person he is must be some further property; and there are obvious relational properties which will do this job. **The Father** is the Father because he has the essential property of **not being caused to exist by anything else** (that is, being ontologically necessary). **The Son** is the Son because he has the essential property of being **caused to exist by an uncaused divine person acting alone**. The Spirit is **the Spirit** because he is **caused to exist by an uncaused divine person in cooperation with a divine person who is caused to exist by the uncaused divine person** acting alone.

Gregory of Nyssa, one of the leading bishops at the Council of Constantinople which formulated the Nicene Creed, wrote, with respect to the difference between the Father and the Son, that 'this is the only way by which we distinguish one [divine] person from another, by believing, that is, that one is the cause and the other depends on the cause' (*Letter to Ablabius*), and he went on to make the point about the Holy Spirit which I have just made. It follows that it was not a matter of chance or voluntary choice of the Father which Son the Father caused to exist when he caused a Son to exist. For any divine person caused to exist solely by the Father would have been the Son. And similarly any divine person caused to exist jointly by Father and Son would have been the Spirit. (By contrast, as I pointed out in Chapter 1, the mere fact that ordinary human parents produce a first or second child does not determine who that first or second child will be; and it still does not do so even when both children have the same genes.) It is only because of this that it is not merely a best kind of act for God the Father to bring about a Son, but a unique best act, for any divine person brought about by God the Father acting alone would have been the same person. And it is not merely a best kind of act for the Father and Son to bring about a Spirit, but a unique best act, for any divine person brought about by Father and Son acting together would have been the same Spirit. If divine persons had thisness, it would depend on chance or the Father's arbitrary choice which further divine persons to bring about; and in that case the ones he did choose would not have existed of metaphysical necessity.

So **why only three divine persons?** Do not these arguments suggest that there should be more than three divine persons, perhaps an infinite number? I claimed in Chapter 1 that when there is a unique best action, God must do that; and when there is a best kind of action, God must do an action of that kind. Now, bringing about the sharing of divinity is a best kind of action and so is bringing about cooperation in sharing of divinity. But there is no comparable best kind of action which would be achieved by bring about a fourth divine person. Bringing about cooperating in sharing with a fourth person is not a qualitatively different kind of good action from bringing about cooperating in sharing with a third person. Or, to use Richard of St Victor's further point, bringing about the Spirit as well as the Son would provide for each divine person someone other than themselves for every other divine person to love and be loved by; but adding **a fourth would not provide a new kind of good state**.

You might think, nevertheless, that, for the above reasons, the more divine persons the better. In that case, since however many divine persons the Father (in conjunction with others) brought about, it would be still better if he brought about more. But, we saw in Chapter 1, when a person has the choice of doing one of a series of incompatible actions, each better than the previous one and no best act, he would be perfectly good if he did any one of these acts. (To bring about only three divine persons would be incompatible with an alternative action of bringing about only four divine persons, and so generally.) So the perfect goodness of the Father would be satisfied by his bringing about only two further divine persons. He does not have to bring about a fourth divine person in order to fulfil his divine nature. But then **any fourth divine person would not exist necessarily**, even in the sense of metaphysical necessity. His existence would not be a necessary consequence of the existence of an ontologically necessary being; and hence he would not be divine. So there cannot be a fourth divine person. There must be and can only be three divine persons. Because it follows necessarily from the existence of one divine person, that there will also be two others, **the hypothesis that there is a Trinity is not more complicated than the hypothesis of theism** for the great simplicity of which I argued in Chapter 1. A simple hypothesis is no less simple for having complicated consequences: all the great simple scientific hypotheses have had many detailed complicated consequences.

Being omniscient, each divine person knows what the other is doing, and, being perfectly good, they give their active causal support to the actions initiated by the others in their spheres of activity. They form a totally integrated divine society, **the Trinity**, which acts as one coordinated whole. This can itself be said to be (in a derivative sense) omnipotent (it can do whatever any member of it chooses), omniscient (each member knows everything logically possible to know), perfectly free (no member is subject to any irrational influences in their choices), and eternal—all of these crucial terms being spelled out in the ways described in Chapter 1. But because in the way described it is a society rather than one person, I shall call it a '**personal being**', and for the rest of this book I shall use the word 'God' as the name of this being. Since, as argued earlier, there can only be three divine persons, there can only be one being of this kind. In this sense there is '**one God**'. So (in a derivative sense) whatever any divine person is and does, God is and does.

How the Creed States the Doctrine of the Trinity

The Nicene Creed expresses the doctrine of the Trinity in the vocabulary of fourth-century Christianity, derived to a considerable degree from the philosophical categories of ancient Greece. I now wish to show briefly that what I have expounded so far largely in my own words is (except in one respect) indeed either the explicit doctrine of the Creed, or the way in which it was uncontroversially understood by later theologians and councils.

The Nicene Creed begins by affirming Christian belief in 'one God'; but goes on to distinguish between 'God the Father', 'one Lord . . . Son of God begotten from the Father . . . true God from true God . . . of one essence with the Father', and 'the Holy Spirit . . . who together with the Father and the Son is worshipped and together glorified'. This is the doctrine that God is a Trinity. The Greek word *theos* (which I've followed most translations in translating as 'God' on each occasion where it occurs in the Creed) may be used either as a proper name for a particular individual and then be properly translated as '**God**', or as a common name for a kind of individual and then be better translated as a '**divine person**'. Since the Creed claims that Father, Son, and Spirit are each *theos* (and so members of the same kind), we should understand this as the claim that they are all divine persons. I shall follow this usage, and mean in future by 'God' used as a proper name 'The Holy Trinity'; and by 'God' used as a common name 'a divine person'. The title of this book is thus asking whether Jesus was a divine person.

Father and Son have the same 'essence'; and later theologians and Church councils spelled out explicitly that the same applied to the Spirit. Generally, the Nicene Creed was seen as committed to the view that each member of the Trinity has each of the divine properties (omnipotence etc.) that I discussed in Chapter I. Thus the fifth-century so-called 'Athanasian Creed', used widely in church worship in the West, affirmed that 'the Father is omnipotent, the Son is omnipotent, the Holy Spirit is omnipotent'. Since each is equally 'to be worshipped and together glorified', each must exist just as inevitably as the others, and so be at least metaphysically necessary. Later theologians and Church councils stated that Father, Son, and Spirit are 'individuals' or 'persons'; but they never said that God (without qualification such as 'God the Father') is a person. So the above claim may be most naturally read as the claim that Father, Son, and Holy Spirit together form one larger individual, God.

The Creed claims that everything began from '**the Father**'. Why call this first divine person 'the Father'? Primarily because (the Bible tells us) Jesus (whom the Creed identifies with 'the Son') addressed the divine person on whom, he clearly believed, everything depended as 'Father'. This name has never been supposed in Christian tradition to imply that the first divine person is male. But it is a natural name for a loving personal source of all other things. Given that, '**the Son**' is a natural name for the second divine person; especially as Jesus often referred to himself as 'Son of God' (although this phrase as used by Jesus did not mean what later Christian theology came to mean by that phrase).

The claim that 'the Son' was '**begotten from the Father**' should be understood simply as the claim that the Son was caused to exist by the Father—which is the same as the claim that he was '**true God from true God**'; no one has been able to give any clear meaning to the word 'begotten' beyond that—it was certainly not meant to imply that the causation involved any sexual process or the joint involvement of a mother. The claim that the Son is 'light from light' is of course to be understood as a highly metaphorical claim. It invokes three apparent features of light: that it helps us to 'see' deep things as they really are, that it spreads itself in all directions with apparently infinite velocity, and (as when one candle is lit by another) does so without ceasing to illuminate places already illuminated. So too, the Creed claims, there is no limit to the illuminating power of the Son which is derived from the illuminating power of the Father without diminishing the latter. The Creed adds that the Son was '**not made**'. For theologians of the fourth century, 'made' meant made out of pre-existing stuff, and the Creed is thus denying that the Son was made out of anything pre-existing.

The Creed calls the third divine person '**the Holy Spirit**', primarily because the Bible several times refers to 'the Holy Spirit' as God's agent in bringing about the birth of Jesus, guiding him in life, and sent by him to guide the Church after Jesus had left the earth. 'Spirit' is a natural word for a being who had this job of 'inspiring'.

The Creed goes on to claim that the Spirit '**proceeds from the Father**'. In the Western Church (which developed into what we now call the Roman Catholic Church) the words 'and the Son' came to be added after 'from the Father', so that the Creed as recited in Catholic and also subsequently in Protestant churches expresses belief in 'the Spirit who proceeds from the Father and the Son'. The Eastern Church (which developed into what we now call the Orthodox Church), as well as the smaller Churches which separated from the Eastern Church (the monophysites and 'Nestorians'), retained the original form. This was not because the Eastern Church wished to deny that the Son played a role in the 'procession' of the Spirit, but because it considered that the Western Church had no right to add these words without the authority of a council of the whole Church. Several of the theologians whom the Eastern Church most reveres affirmed a role for the Son in the 'procession' of the Spirit, by claiming that the Spirit proceeds from the Father 'through the Son'. No one has been able to give any sense to 'proceeds from' except as meaning 'was caused by', and so no one has been able to make any clear distinction between 'being begotten by' and 'proceeding from'. Since clearly the Son can only help to bring about the Spirit in virtue of the nature which the Father gives him, I cannot see that there is any difference between 'proceeds from the Father and the Son' and 'proceeds from the Father through the Son'.

However, the Creed is certainly not committed to the view that the Son is involved in the procession of the Spirit, and many Orthodox theologians have denied it. I did, however, give earlier what I regard as a strong argument in favour of the involvement of the Son in the procession of the Spirit, that the love of Father and Son required them to cooperate in bringing about a third divine person.

The Creed claims that the Son was 'begotten from the Father' **'before all ages'**; and the Council of Ephesus (AD 431) and subsequent councils and theologians made it clear that this meant that the Son was eternal, like the Father; as with the Father, there was no time at which the Son did not exist. Other councils and theologians made it clear that the same applied to the Spirit. The Father causing the existence of the Son, and (with or through the Son) the existence of the Spirit, is therefore to be read as the Father causing their existence at each moment of unending time, always keeping them in existence. The Creed also indicates, as I have suggested that we should expect, that the three members of the Trinity have at any time different spheres of activity. It speaks of God the Father who is '**maker of Heaven and earth, and of all things both seen and unseen'**. It claims that the process of creating everything apart from himself (which is how 'Heaven and earth and all things seen and unseen' is to be read) began with the Father. At each moment, when anything exists apart from God, it exists because the Father is causing it to exist; every such thing is either an already existing thing which the Father keeps in existence or a new thing which he brings into existence. He **made everything 'through the Son'**; that is, the way in which he causes things to exist is by directing the Son to cause them to exist. The Son '**became incarnate'** and lived on earth, and **will 'come again in glory to judge the living and the dead'**. The Spirit is 'the giver of life', that is, causes inanimate things to become alive (and gives souls to human bodies); and he also '**spoke through the prophets'**, that is, inspired the prophets of ancient Israel to preach their message. I conclude that the Trinity for which I have given a priori arguments is the Trinity of the Nicene Creed, although that

Creed does need to be filled out in one possible way rather than a different one.

The argument which I have given in this chapter for the necessity of God being a Trinity may seem a very sophisticated one. But it **depends on two very simple moral intuitions**: that perfect love requires total sharing with an equal and requires cooperating in spreading that love further, so that anyone you love has someone else to love and be loved by. The first of these intuitions was, I think, one of the two reasons why Christians came to believe this doctrine. (The second intuition had to wait a thousand years for someone to state it explicitly.) **The other reason** why Christians came to believe the doctrine was, they held, that **the doctrine had been revealed** by the teaching of Jesus recorded in the New Testament and proclaimed as central Christian doctrine by the Church which he founded. I shall be arguing in due course that we also have this latter reason.

3 GOD SHARED OUR HUMAN NATURE

God Had to Share Our Human Suffering

It is an obvious general fact about the world that humans not merely suffer but do much wrong. How will a loving God respond to the suffering and wrongdoing of these feeble but partly rational creatures whom he has made? I will argue in this chapter that a priori we would expect God to respond to our suffering and wrongdoing by himself living a human life. God would live a human life by one divine person becoming human (that is, 'becoming incarnate'). I will argue in this chapter that God would inevitably live a human life in order to share human suffering; and I will argue in the next two chapters that quite probably God would use that human life in order to make available atonement for our wrongdoing and to teach us how to live. When I have spelled out why God needed to become incarnate in order to share our suffering, it will become clear that he would need to become incarnate in a particular way in order to do this. Then in the rest of the chapter I shall show that the Christian doctrine of how God became incarnate has the consequence that he became incarnate in the right kind of way.

As Christian thinkers have normally maintained, God had no obligation to create a world (for if he failed to do so, there would not ever have been any creatures who had been wronged). It was not even—I claimed in Chapter 1—a unique best act to create a world containing humans who suffer and do wrong: either to create such a world or not to create one seem to me equal best acts. Because of the goodness of there being creatures with free choices between good and evil who can mould their characters for good or ill, it would be a good act to create it. Because of the suffering inevitably involved in such a world, it would have been equally good for God not to create it. But, I shall be arguing, it would have been a generous act for God to create humans, in view of the obligation which thereby God imposed upon himself.

Because of the goodness of humans having free choices, God
has—I claimed in Chapter 1—a good reason to allow them to
hurt each other; and good reason to allow them to suffer pains
caused by disease and accident in order to allow them more
significant choices and thereby form their own characters. We
ordinary **humans sometimes rightly subject our own children
to suffering** for the sake of some greater good (to themselves or
others); for instance (to use my earlier example) make them attend
a 'difficult' neighbourhood school for the sake of good community
relations. Under these circumstances it is a good thing if we show
solidarity with our children by putting ourselves in somewhat the
same situation as they are: for example, by becoming involved
in the parent–teacher organization of their neighbourhood school.
Sometimes we may need to subject our children to serious suffering
for the sake of a greater good to others; and then there comes a
point at which it is not merely good but obligatory to show
solidarity with the sufferer. Suppose that, my country has been
unjustly attacked, and the government has introduced conscription
in order to raise an army to defend the country. All young men
between 18 and 30 are 'called up' to serve in the army; older men
under 50 may volunteer. The government however allows parents
of those aged between 18 and 21 to 'veto' a call-up. Suppose that
I have a 19-year old son; and, although most parents veto their
young sons 'call up', I refuse to do so because of the gravity of
the threat to the country's independence. Suppose also that I am
45 years old, and so have no legal obligation to serve. Plausibly
since I am forcing my son to endure the hardship and danger of
military service, I have a moral obligation to him to volunteer
myself. In circumstances of this kind the sharing must not be
entirely incognito. The parent needs not merely to share the child's
suffering, but to show him that he is doing so. Hence it seems
to me highly plausible to suppose that, given the amount of pain
and suffering which God allows humans to endure (for a good
purpose), it would be **obligatory on God to share a human life
of suffering**. This would be achieved by a divine person becoming
incarnate as a human (that is, becoming a human being) and living
a life containing much suffering ending with the great crisis which
all humans have to face: the crisis of death. And an obvious way in
which that divine person, whom I shall now call 'God Incarnate',
could share the worst suffering which humans endure would be

for him to live a life which ended with a painful and unjustly imposed death.

And not merely would God have an obligation to live a human life of suffering, but **God would have to show us that he had done this**: the Incarnation would not serve its purpose if humans did not learn about it. Given that the human life of God Incarnate would be of limited duration, he must provide a way of informing the future human race throughout the world of what he had done—and that means that **he must found a Church** which, he would ensure, would proclaim this message. (I'll develop this point in Chapter 5.)

How God Could Become Human?

But how could a divine person who is essentially divine, that is omnipotent, omniscient, perfectly free, eternal, and so metaphysically necessary, become human? To be human is to have a human way of thinking and acting and (at least normally) a human body through which to act. Being **essentially divine**, he could not cease to be divine. So a divine person could only become human by **acquiring a human way of thinking and acting and a human body** in addition to his divine way of thinking and acting. Although God does not need a body, he could acquire one, and this body would be uniquely his in that he was the only person to act through it.

What makes a way of thinking **a human way of thinking**? In contrast to animals, humans are capable of logical thought, among their beliefs are moral beliefs (beliefs about which actions are good or bad, obligatory or wrong), and they have free will. But clearly normal humans have these qualities in only a limited degree: their logical powers are fairly primitive, their moral beliefs (like all their other beliefs) are of limited scope and sometimes false, and their freedom (as I commented in Chapter 1) is very limited. Their desires are of a characteristically human kind, some of them, such as desires for food, drink, sleep, and sex, largely of genetic origin; and some of them, including perhaps desires for fame and fortune, largely the result of cultural influences. Humans have **a body** when they acquire their beliefs through their bodies (from what they perceive and from what others tell them), and seek to realize their purposes through their bodies (by moving mouths, arms, legs, etc.).

So how could a divine person acquire this human way of thinking with its accompanying body in addition to but separate from his own essential divine way of thinking? It was **Freud,** the modern founder of psychoanalysis, who helped us to see how a person can have two systems of belief to some extent independent of each other. Freud described people who sometimes, when performing some actions, act only on one system of beliefs and are not guided by beliefs of the other system; and conversely. Although all the beliefs of such a person are accessible to him, he refuses to admit to his consciousness the beliefs of the one system when he is acting in the light of the other system of beliefs. Thus, to take a well-worn example, a mother may refuse to acknowledge to herself a belief that her son is dead or to allow some of her actions to be guided by it. When asked if she believes that he is dead, she says 'No', and this is an honest reply, for it is guided by those beliefs of which she is conscious. Yet other actions of hers may be guided by the belief that her son is dead (even though she does not admit that belief to consciousness); for instance, she may throw away some of his possessions. The refusal to admit a belief to consciousness is of course itself also something that the mother refuses to admit to herself to be happening.

The Freudian account of the divided mind was derived from analysis of cases of human self-deception, where a person does not consciously acknowledge either the beliefs of one belief system or the belief that he has kept its beliefs separated from his other system, and where the self-deception is a pathetic state from which that person needs to be rescued. But the Freudian account of such cases helps us to see the possibility of a person intentionally keeping a lesser belief system separate from her main belief system, and simultaneously doing different actions guided by different sets of beliefs, of both of which she is consciously aware—all for some very good reason. Indeed even people who do not suffer from a Freudian divided mind can sometimes perform simultaneously two quite separate tasks (for example, having a conversation with someone and writing a letter to someone else) in directing which quite distinct beliefs are involved, which we can recognize as 'on the way to' a divided mind in which we have two different sets of beliefs.

Now a divine person could not give up his knowledge and so his beliefs, for his omniscience is one of his essential properties—without it he would not exist; but in becoming incarnate he could allow himself to have **a separate system of semi-beliefs** in the sense of propositions which he would believe if he did not have the divine beliefs. These semi-beliefs would be caused in him by the stimuli landing on the eyes, ears, etc. of his human body in the same way as full beliefs are caused in us; and they would interact in the same way in him as our beliefs do in us to produce an integrated world-view. I shall in future call these semi-beliefs **God Incarnate's human 'beliefs'**. He would do different actions in the light of different belief systems. The actions done through his human body, the thoughts consciously entertained connected with the human brain, the interpretation of perceptual data acquired through the human eyes, would all be done in the light of the human belief system. So, too, would any public statement made through his human mouth. However, his divine belief system will inevitably include the knowledge that his human system contains the beliefs that it does; and it will itself also contain those among the latter beliefs which are true. The separation of the belief systems would be a voluntary act, knowledge of which was part of God Incarnate's divine belief system but not of his human belief system. We thus get a picture of **a divine consciousness and a human consciousness of God Incarnate**, the divine consciousness including the human consciousness, but the human consciousness not including the divine consciousness.

The beliefs in the two parts of a divided mind may sometimes be explicitly contradictory, for example, the mother's belief that her son is alive and her belief that her son is dead. In such a case, it is misleading to call both beliefs 'beliefs' without qualification, since at least one does not form part of a general view of the world but merely guides the subject's actions in certain circumstances. The overall constant and ever-present view of the world of a God who became incarnate in the way described would be his divine view; and so the 'beliefs' belonging to that view are truly 'beliefs', whereas the 'beliefs' belonging to the human perspective would be mere semi-beliefs guiding a limited set of actions. But it would be the 'beliefs' belonging to the human perspective which would guide the honest public statements of God Incarnate (honest, because guided by those beliefs of which he is conscious in his human acting).

The human acts of God Incarnate would be the public acts done through his human body and the private mental acts correlated with the brain-states of that body, and if it is to be a human body its capacities must not be radically different from those of our bodies. So there would be a limit to the power of God Incarnate *as* a human. If his human actions were done only in the light of his human beliefs, then he would feel the limitations that we have. In becoming incarnate, God would not have limited his powers, but he **would have taken on an additional limited way of operating**. So, using the notion of the divided mind, we can coherently suppose a divine person to become incarnate while remaining divine, and yet act and feel much like ourselves.

God Incarnate would also acquire human desires—for fame and fortune as well as for food and drink. Desires, we saw in Chapter 1, incline us to do actions; and desires of the kinds to which humans are subject often incline us to do actions which are bad or less than the best. As I noted in Chapter 1, people only have a free choice between (what they believe to be) the best and (what they believe to be) bad or less than the best, if they are subject to desires (natural inclinations) to do (what they believe to be) bad or less than the best stronger than their desires to do (what they believe to be) best. Does this mean that God Incarnate would have been able to do wrong?

Wrong is of two kinds: **objective** and **subjective**. Objective wrong is failing in your obligations (or duties) to someone whether you realize it or not; for example, taking money that belongs to someone else, whether or not you believe that it belongs to someone else. Subjective wrong, the more serious kind of wrong, is doing (or trying to do) an action which you believe involves failing in your obligations to someone, for example, taking money which you believe to belong to someone else; and for that you are blameworthy or culpable. In both cases, a wrong is a wrong to someone. If you take what belongs to someone else, you wrong the person from whom you take it. If you take something, believing that you are taking what belongs to someone else, you wrong the person from whom you believe that you are taking it. If God were to fail in any of his duties to humans, he would wrong them. He would wrong a human objectively if, for instance, he failed to keep a promise to him, whether or not he realized that he was failing to fulfil the duty. He would wrong a human subjectively if he did what he believed was failing in his duty to him.

Now it would, I suggest, have been wrong of a divine person to allow himself to become incarnate in such a way as to open the possibility of his doing objective or subjective wrong. For it is wrong of anyone to put themselves in a position where they are liable to do wrong to someone—intentionally allow themselves to forget their duties, or to take drugs which would lead to their being strongly tempted to do some wrong, or simply be unable to stop themselves from doing wrong. That is why it is wrong to drive a car when you have drunk too much alcohol: you put yourself in a position where you are likely to kill or injure others. It follows from God's essential perfect freedom and omniscience that he would not put himself in a position where he could have chosen to do wrong. So in becoming incarnate God must have ensured that in his human actions he had access to such true moral beliefs as would allow him to be aware of his duties, and he must have ensured that he would never be subject to too strong a desire to do any action which was wrong. Even though **God Incarnate could not do wrong**, he may, however, through not allowing himself to be aware of his divine beliefs, have been inclined to believe that he might succumb to temptation to do wrong and thus, in the situation of temptation, **he could have *felt* as we do.**

While it is wrong to put oneself in a position where one is liable to do wrong, there is nothing wrong in putting oneself in a position where one is liable not to do the best action (or equal best or best or equal best kind of action) or even a bad action (if there are any bad actions which are not wrong). Indeed, an action which had the foreseen consequence of putting oneself in that position might itself occasionally be the best thing to do. A generous person might well, as a supererogatory good act, give away so much money that she would be so short of money in future that she would be much tempted not to do any more supererogatory good acts. Yet, as I defined 'perfect freedom' in Chapter 1, a perfectly free person is one subject to no irrational desires. From that it follows that he would inevitably do what he believed to be the best action if he believed that there was a best action. But I now insert a qualification into this definition which I did not introduce in Chapter 1 in order to keep the exposition there as simple as possible. **I now define a perfectly free person** as one subject to no irrational desires except in so far as, uninfluenced by such desires, he chooses to allow himself to act while being influenced by such desires (though not compelled to yield to them). This preserves the point of the original definition that such a person is at the highest level uninfluenced by any considerations except those of reason in determining how he will act, but allows that he may rationally choose to allow himself to do certain acts while open to the influence of irrational desires. So, on this understanding of perfect freedom, **God Incarnate could have chosen at a time to allow himself to make his choice at that time under the influence of temptation to do less than the best.** He would then have needed to fight against the temptation not to do that best action; and it would have been possible that he would yield to that temptation and done instead a less good action (and perhaps even a bad action, though certainly not a wrong action). He might choose to put himself in the situation of temptation of this kind in order to share our human condition as fully as possible. If in his human consciousness God Incarnate were on occasion subject to a balance of desire (a strong temptation) not to do the best action, then his overcoming this temptation would be a free act for which he would be praiseworthy.

It might be that in his human thinking God Incarnate was **not always conscious of his own divinity**; but he would clearly need to be conscious of it some of the time in order to show his followers that he believed himself to be divine, and so to give them good reason to believe that God had identified with our suffering.

In summary, then, in becoming incarnate a divine person must remain omniscient, but he could allow his human actions to be guided only by his humanly acquired inclinations to belief. He must remain omnipotent, but there is a limit to what he could do in a human way and, when he acts in a human way, he need not always be fully aware of having more power than that. Being divine, he must remain perfectly free, but he could, in perfect freedom and because of the perfect goodness of doing so, allow himself to make a choice under the influence of a desire to do a lesser good. God Incarnate could not do wrong. He could, nevertheless, feel as we do when we are tempted to do wrong, and he could have been tempted to do acts other than the best ones available. He could have yielded to these latter temptations; and if he did any supererogatory acts he would probably do them by resisting such temptations.

The Doctrine of the Incarnation

The Christian doctrine of the Incarnation claims that God did become incarnate in just this kind of way; God the Son became God Incarnate. The Nicene Creed affirms that God the Son, the second person of the Trinity, 'came down from the heavens, and was incarnate. . . . and became human'. **'Came down from the heavens'** must not be read in the literal sense of descending from the sky; for the Gospels (which those who formulated the Creed regarded as the source of their doctrine) record no such 'descent', and all Christians believed that God was omnipresent, present everywhere. Rather, 'came down' must be read metaphorically as 'acquired a lower status' (as a human, that is); and 'from the heavens' must be read as 'than his status as divine'. He **'became human'**; and when he was born, he was given the name of Jesus. The fact of the birth of God the Son as a human (Jesus Christ) at a particular time is a quite different fact from the eternal dependence of God the Son on God the Father.

The Nicene Creed gave no explanation of what God becoming human involved. But in AD 451 the later Council of Chalcedon gave an explanation. It taught that God the Son continued throughout his earthly life and thereafter to have a **divine nature** (*physis*) which he had always had. But he acquired at his conception also a **human nature**. He was (after his conception) a single **individual** (*hypostasis*) with two distinct natures. This **'Chalcedonian definition'**, as it is called, was accepted by the considerable majority of Christians, both by those who came to form the Roman Catholic and Orthodox churches, and (at the Reformation) by most Protestants. The form of words, 'two *physes*', 'one *hypostasis*', which the Council adopted was, however, rejected by two groups: the monophysites and the 'Nestorians'. The **monophysites** (today's Copts and some other quite large Middle Eastern groups) held that Jesus had only one *physis*, while the **'Nestorians'** (today's Church of the East, a small Middle Eastern group) held that in Jesus there were two *hypostases*. Whether the disagreement of these two groups with the Chalcedonian definition was a difference of substance or a mere difference of words depends on whether all those involved meant the same by the two technical terms. Discussions in the last twenty years between the official representatives of monophysite churches and official representatives of the Orthodox Church, and between official representatives of the Church of the East and the Roman Catholic Church, have established that, at any rate today, there is no substantial disagreement on the part of either monophysite churches or the Church of the East with the doctrine which Catholics and Orthodox understood to be expressed by the Chalcedonian definition; the monophysite churches and the Church of the East oppose the definition because they understand the Greek words in different senses. So, while I shall spell out the Chalcedonian definition in a way accepted by Catholics and Orthodox, what I spell out will be a doctrine acceptable to all of these groups.

So understood, a *hypostasis* is an individual thing (in the sense used in Chapter 1, a substance), and a rational *hypostasis* is a **person**. Divine persons and human persons are persons in the sense that they are individuals who have beliefs and powers (of some sophistication) and choose freely which actions to perform. Jesus Christ is one person; he is not two persons closely bound together. But he has two natures. Natures are properties of things. An essential nature or essence of a thing are the thing's essential properties, those which it has to have in order to exist at all. Jesus's divine nature is an essential nature. He has essentially the divine properties, discussed in previous chapters, of omnipotence, omniscience, etc. which make him divine; and the further property which makes him the particular divine person he is, the Son, the property of being caused to exist only by the Father.

But, the Chalcedonian definition claims, God the Son also acquired at his conception in the womb of Mary a human nature. This nature is therefore a contingent nature; Jesus did not need to have it in order to exist. The Council of Chalcedon spelled out having a human nature as having 'a **rational soul** and a body'. There were two possible ways of understanding a 'soul' familiar to those who participated in the Council of Chalcedon: Plato's understanding and Aristotle's understanding. For Plato the soul is the essential part of a person which makes a person the particular person he or she is; it is a part which can be separated from the person's body (if he or she has a body). For Aristotle a soul is not a part of a person; but is a way of thinking and acting possessed by a person—in the terms of Chapter 1, a property of a person. On Aristotle's view a human soul is just the way a human body thinks and behaves, and it is having this way of thinking and acting which makes the body a human being. The Council bishops must be understood to be using the term 'soul' in Aristotle's sense, for God the Son could not acquire a new soul of Plato's kind since a soul of that kind is what makes the individual who has it the person he is, and the Son was already constituted as the person he is by his divine properties. Rather, the Council must be understood as saying that God the Son acquired a new way of thinking and acting. 'Rational' must be read as 'human'. Human souls were often described in ancient thought as 'rational' souls, to distinguish them from the souls of animals, which were not capable of rational thought but were capable only of having sensations. The Council was certainly not denying that a divine nature was supremely rational; rather, in acquiring a 'rational' soul, the Son was acquiring a human kind of rationality, that is, a human way of thinking and acting in addition to his divine way of thinking and acting.

Chalcedon claims (as I have translated it, following the normal translation) that God the Son became '**like us in all respects except for wrongdoing**'. Chalcedon is claiming that Jesus, God the Son, did not do wrong to anyone. I argued earlier that God must become incarnate in such a way as not to allow him to do wrong. But that is compatible with his doing less than the best. It would then follow that, given that he always did the best or equal best action (where there was a best or equal best action), he might have done it despite the temptation to do otherwise to which he could have yielded. Christian tradition claims that the life of Jesus was a perfect life; and we should understand by that a life in which he did no bad actions, many good actions, and always did the best or equal best action or kind of action where there was one available.

The Creed tells us that Jesus '**was crucified**', and so died; that in the process he '**suffered**'; and that then he '**was buried**'. I conclude that the Creed, as filled out by the Chalcedonian definition claims that Jesus God Incarnate led a human life involving much of the kind of suffering that the most unfortunate human beings have to suffer. Thereby God would have fulfilled the obligation which he imposed on himself in creating humans who have to suffer for the sake of a greater good.

While inevitably that life would be free from wrongdoing, I shall be arguing in the next chapter that it would need to be a perfect life if God was to achieve another possible goal of his incarnation. A perfect life need not end in a death by execution, but those who protest too strongly against injustice, above all if they claim divine authority for their actions, were very likely to get executed in many ancient societies. If God is to live a perfect life sharing our suffering, it is plausible to suppose that he might choose to live in a society where it is highly probable that living a perfect life pays the highest price—death by execution.

The Virgin Birth

The Nicene Creed also affirms a doctrine about how God the Son became incarnate, 'from the Holy Spirit and the Virgin Mary'. This doctrine of the Virgin Birth claims that God the Holy Spirit caused Mary, the mother of Jesus, to conceive Jesus without that conception involving any sperm from a male human; Jesus had no human father. While the union of a particular male sperm and a particular female egg gives rise to a fertilized egg with a full set of genes and so eventually to a new human being, it in no way affects who that human will be. Our genes have a powerful influence on the kind of person we become—our physiology, our appearance, and our character; but, as I argued in Chapter 1, they have no influence on *who* acquires those genes. And so, if God had so chosen, God the Son could have been born of two human parents. But the claim is that Jesus had only a mother. Since he had, to all appearances, normal human bodily characteristics, he presumably had a full set of chromosomes and so genes such as normal humans derive from two parents. The Creed has nothing to say about such matters (and, of course, those who wrote the Creed knew nothing about chromosomes and genes). But it would not have taken a very large miracle for God to turn some of the material of Mary's egg into a second half-set of chromosomes, which, together with the normal half-set derived from Mary, would provide a full set.

But is there any **a priori reason** for supposing that, if God was to become incarnate, he would choose to do so by means of a 'virgin birth'? It would mean that Jesus came into existence as a human on earth partly by the normal process by which all humans come into existence, and partly as a result of a quite abnormal process. It would thus be a historical event symbolizing the doctrine of the Incarnation, that Jesus is partly of human origin and so has a human nature, and partly of divine origin and so has a divine nature. This event would help those who learnt about it later to understand the doctrine of the Incarnation. That God should bring about a historical event which symbolized what was happening at a deeper level seems to me to have a fairly low but not totally insignificant degree of prior probability.

The Ascension

The Creed claims that at the end of his life on earth Jesus 'ascended into the heavens'. Since 'coming down from the heavens' is clearly to be understood in the way described at the beginning of the chapter as 'acquired a lower status', 'ascended into the heavens' should be understood as 'abandoned his lower status'. He no longer lived as a human on earth, and no longer had human thoughts of a kind which involved no awareness of his divinity. Since the purposes for which God would have become incarnate, one of which I have considered in this chapter and others which I shall consider in subsequent chapters, require him to live only one human life, an ascension in this sense is **a priori highly probable**. (Although this is no part of the Creed, the later Church generally claimed that Jesus retained his human nature and body subsequent to his Ascension. If so, that body must occupy a place, in that 'Heaven' in which—see Chapter 6—Christianity claims that the good dead will live.) The Ascension may of course have been symbolized, as some books of the New Testament claim, by his body rising upwards into the sky until covered by a cloud. In the story of the Exodus in the Old Testament, as in the New Testament story of the 'transfiguration of Jesus', God manifested his presence by means of a cloud. Jesus rising into the sky would thus symbolize a return to God. (The Christian Bible consists of two parts: the Old Testament, largely concerned with the history of ancient Israel and its relations with God, and the New Testament, concerned with the life and teaching of Jesus and the early Church which he founded.) Jesus became again united to his Father as fully as could be. And that, since there is no sense in which the Father has a spatial location, is how the claim that the Son is 'seated at the right hand of the Father' is to be understood. By the customs of the ancient world, as well as of the modern world, the honoured agent of a president's policy would sit at the president's right hand when present at a meeting.

In this chapter I have given one a priori reason for believing that God would become a human being: in creating human beings who suffer (for a good reason) as much as we do, he incurred an obligation to share our human life including that suffering. I have tried to make sense of how God could become human; and I have shown that the way in which I have done this was the way in which the Council of Chalcedon claimed that God had become incarnate in Jesus. I have given a reason why God might become incarnate by means of a 'virgin birth', and bring his life on earth to an end with an 'ascension'—as the Creed claims that he did. In the next two chapters I shall give two further reasons why we might expect God to become incarnate.

4 GOD ATONED FOR OUR WRONGDOING

Humans suffer—and, I claimed in the previous chapter, for that reason God needed to become incarnate, in order to share that suffering. But humans have also greatly wronged God. Wronging God is called '**sinning**'. God needed to react to human sin. There is more than one way in which he could do this; but one way in which he could react is by providing atonement for that sin. It is in this way, Christianity claims, that he did react.

Human Sin

I pointed out in Chapter 1 that there are two sorts of good actions: obligatory actions and supererogatory good actions. Obligations are obligations to someone. I have an obligation to you if I am talking to you to tell you only what is true; I have an obligation to my children to feed and educate my children. When we fail in our obligations, we wrong those to whom we had or believed we had the obligation. I pointed out in Chapter 3 that wronging is of two kinds. I wrong you objectively if I do not repay the money which I borrowed from you, even if I had forgotten that I had borrowed it (and even if it is not my fault that I had forgotten). I wrong you subjectively if I believe that I have borrowed money from you and do not repay it. And, of course, much wrongdoing is both objective and subjective, as when I do not repay money which I have borrowed and believe that I have borrowed. By objective wrongdoing, I acquire what I shall call **objective guilt**; and by subjective wrongdoing I acquire what I shall call **subjective guilt**. Obviously, subjective guilt is the worse kind of guilt since it results from knowingly chosen action. It is a stain on the soul, and needs to be dealt with. We are culpable, blameworthy for our subjective wrongdoing. But objective guilt matters also. If I have not repaid money I owe you, there is still something amiss with me even if I have forgotten about my debt; and it needs to be dealt with. In interacting with other people we accept responsibility for our obligations to them, and an unintended failure to perform these obligations involves (non-culpable) guilt. I shall call dealing with our guilt 'making atonement' for our wrongdoing.

Atonement has four components: repentance, apology, reparation, and penance, not all of which are required to remove objective guilt or the subjective guilt arising from less serious wrongdoing. If I wrong you, I must make **reparation** for the effects of my wrongdoing. If I have stolen your watch, I must return it and compensate you for the inconvenience and trauma resulting from my thieving. If the watch has been destroyed, I must give you back something of equivalent value. When I have deprived you of a service I owe you, I must perform the service and compensate you for the delay. But what needs to be dealt with is not merely the effects of wrongdoing; there is also the fact of wrongdoing—that I have sought to hurt you. I must distance myself from that as far as can be done. I do this by sincere **apology**; and that, where the wrongdoing is subjective, involves not only an apology but inner **repentance** as well. But for serious wrongdoing, mere words of apology are often not enough. I need to show you my repentance by doing something extra for you, doing for you more than is needed to compensate for the effects of my wrongdoing. I may give you a small gift, or provide an extra service as a token of my sorrow; and I shall call doing this making a **penance**. Where the guilt is only objective, repentance is not required (I cannot repent of something for which I am not to blame); and where the wrongdoing is not serious, there is less need of penance. The process is completed when the **wronged person** (or victim), agrees to treat the **wrongdoer**, in so far as he can, as one who has not wronged him; and to do that is to **forgive** him. Forgiving is often done by saying the words 'I forgive you'.

It is not necessary, in order for the victim to forgive the wrongdoer, that the latter should make a full atonement. Some apology and (if the wrong is subjective) repentance is always required, but the victim can determine how much (if any) reparation is required. I may let the wrongdoer off the need to compensate me for stealing my watch, if he has destroyed it and has no money with which to repay me—so long as he apologizes, and the apology sounds sincere (that is, sounds as if it is backed by repentance). It is, however, bad, I suggest, to treat someone who has wronged you seriously and yet does not even attempt to make a sincere apology as one who has not wronged you. It is not to take his hostile stance towards you seriously; it is to treat him as a child not responsible for his actions. If someone has killed your much-loved wife and yet for some reason is beyond the reach of the law, it would be bad simply to ignore this and to enjoy his company at a party; it would be insulting to your wife to do so. Since forgiving is a good thing, I suggest that we only call treating the wrongdoer as one who has not wronged you 'forgiving' him where it is good so to treat him, that is, when treating him in this way is a response at least to some apparent repentance and apology on his part. Without this, treating the wrongdoer as someone who has not wronged you is condoning his wrong actions.

Now it is, I suggest, an obvious general fact that almost all humans have wronged God, directly and indirectly; that is, all have sinned. We wrong him directly when we fail to pay him proper worship. Deep reverence and gratitude is owed to the holy source of our existence. We wrong him indirectly when we wrong any of his creatures, the humans and animals whom he has created. For thereby we abuse the free will and responsibility we have been given by God—and to misuse a gift is to wrong the giver. And in wronging God's creatures, we wrong God also in virtue of the fact that he created these creatures. If I hit your child, I wrong you, for I damage a person on whom you have exercised your loving care. Such wronging is **actual sin**—sometimes only objective but often subjective as well, at least in the respect that the wrongdoer believes that he is doing wrong to someone, even if he does not realize that he is doing wrong to God. But it is, of course, far worse if he realizes that he is wronging the good God who created him and keeps him in being from moment to moment.

But there is more to our bad condition than mere actual sin. There is an element inherited from our ancestors and ultimately from our first human ancestor, whom—defined as the first of our ancestors who had free will and moral concepts—we may call Adam. We inherit a proneness to wrongdoing which (in view of the fact that all wrongdoing involves wronging God, at least indirectly) I shall call **original sinfulness**. Our original sinfulness consists of the bad desires which we have inherited from our ancestors, especially desires to seek our immediate well-being in lesser respects at the expense of others and at the expense of our ultimate well-being.

This inheritance is partly 'social'. If our parents behave badly, that influences us to behave badly. But the inheritance is also genetic. We inherit our ancestors' genes, which cause our strong desires to seek far more than our fair share of food, sleep, shelter, sex, etc.; and evidence has emerged within the last two years that what a person does and what other people do to him at an early age affects the genes he or she hands on to their children. (For example, if boys smoke a lot before puberty, that affects their genes in such a way that their children tend to be more obese than they would be otherwise. See *New Scientist*, 7 January 2006. Obesity clearly makes certain good actions harder to do.)

But, as well as inheriting original sinfulness, we also inherit something analogous to the guilt of our actual sin. All our ancestors have done wrong, and in consequence they owe God atonement; but they have not (or at least most of them have not) made that atonement: it still needs to be made. We are indebted to our ancestors for our life and so many of the good things which come to us. For God in creating us has acted through our ancestors, who have not merely brought us into the world, but often lavished much care on our nurture or on the nurture of our parents or their parents etc. from which we have ultimately benefited. Those who have received great benefit from others owe them a smaller benefit in return. What we could do (in theory) for our ancestors is to help with their atonement. We who have inherited from them so much positive good have inherited also a debt. Even the English law requires that before you can claim what you inherit from your dead parents you must pay their debts. To inherit a debt is not to inherit guilt. For we were not the agents of our ancestors' wrongdoing, but we have inherited a responsibility to make atonement for this debt of 'original sin', as far as we can—perhaps by making some reparation.

It is beginning to look as if we humans are in no very good position to make proper atonement for sins, despite having an obligation to make that atonement. We owe so much anyway by way of service to God our creator, who has given us so much. We owe a lot more in virtue of our own actual sins; and yet more in virtue of the sins of our ancestors. And yet, because of the size of the debt and because of our own original sinfulness, it would be very difficult for us to make any proper atonement. How would a good God react to this situation? One possibility is that God could help us to make proper atonement.

How God Could Help Us to Make Atonement

How can someone else help us to make atonement? 'No one can atone for the sins of another.' Taken literally, that remains profoundly true. You cannot make my apologies, or even pay my debts. If I steal $100 from John and you give him an equivalent sum, he has not lost money; but it remains the case that I still owe $100 to John. But one human can help another to make the necessary atonement—can persuade him to repent, help him to formulate the words of an apology, and give him the means by which to make reparation and penance.

So what would be a proper reparation (and penance) for us to offer to God if someone else provided the means of reparation? What has gone wrong is that we humans have lived bad human lives. A proper offering would be a perfect human life which might well—I argued in Chapter 3—end in a death by execution, which we can offer to God as our reparation. Maybe one human life, however perfect, would not equate in quantity of goodness to the badness of so many human lives. But it is up to the wronged person to deem when a sufficient reparation has been made; and one truly perfect life would surely be a proper amount of reparation for God to deem that reparation (and penance) enough had been made.

I argued in Chapter 3 that God had an obligation to lead a human life of suffering, in order to show solidarity with our suffering. In that life he could do no wrong. But he would have no obligation to live a perfect life (that is, one in which he did no bad actions, many good actions, and always did the best or equal best action or kind of action, where there was one). He could have been subject to temptation not to live such a life, and it would have been good that he should allow himself to be thus tempted in order that if he succeeded, his success would have resulted from overcoming temptation when ordinary humans often yield to temptation. Thus it would have been a life of the kind that God wished each of us to live. God could then make that life available to us as our reparation. (And if he had yielded to temptation, and failed to live a perfect life, he could have become incarnate a second time and tried again. Sooner or later he could likely have provided for us that perfect life which ones serve as our reparation.) If a wrongdoer has no means to make reparation, a well-wisher may often provide him with the means; the wrongdoer can then choose whether or not to use that means for that purpose. Suppose that I owe you some service; for example, suppose that I have promised to clean your house and that you have already paid me to do this. Suppose also that I have spent the money but omitted to clean the house at the promised time, and that I have now had an accident which makes me unable to clean the house. Clearly I owe you repentance and apology; but I must also try to get someone else to clean the house. Even if you don't badly need the house to be cleaned, you may think it important that I should be involved in getting it cleaned; it matters that I should take responsibility for what I have omitted to do. So you may encourage a third person to offer to me to clean the house on my behalf. If I accept this offer, I am involved in providing the reparation; and when the house is cleared, you can forgive me.

The Christian Doctrine of the Atonement

The Nicene Creed affirms that God the Son became incarnate as Jesus '**for us humans and for our salvation**'. Passages of different books of the New Testament spell this out in terms of claims that Jesus '**saved us from our sins**'. There is in Christian tradition no one agreed account of the doctrine of the Atonement, that is, of *how* Jesus by his life and death made atonement for our sins; whereas, as we have seen, that tradition does contain agreed accounts of the doctrines of the Trinity and the Incarnation.

I suggest that the Christian claim that Jesus saved us from our sins may be best understood in the way that I have suggested: God could help us to make atonement for our sins and those of our ancestors. By becoming incarnate and living a perfect human life in Jesus, God provided an act of reparation of which we can avail ourselves. God was both the wronged person (the victim of our wrongdoing) and also the one who, thinking it so important that we should take our wrongdoing seriously, made available the reparation for us to offer back to him. Or, more precisely, we have sinned against God the Father, our ultimate creator; and it is God the Son who makes available the reparation. My account coincides with the account of the Atonement which is given both by the Letter to the Hebrews, which is the book of the New Testament which gives the fullest account of this doctrine, and also by St Thomas Aquinas, the medieval thinker who has influenced so much of the subsequent theology of Western Christendom.

The Letter to the Hebrews speaks of Jesus offering a sacrifice of himself, 'to bear the sins of many' (Heb. 9: 28). In the most primitive way of thinking about sacrifice lying behind (the far more sophisticated) Old Testament thought, a sacrifice is the giving of something valuable to a God, who consumes it by inhaling the smoke, and often gives back some of it to be consumed by the worshippers (who eat some of the flesh of the sacrificed animal). The sacrifice of Jesus is then Jesus (God the Son) giving to God (the Father) the most valuable thing he has: his life—both a perfect life of service to God and humans in difficult circumstances, and a life which he allowed to be taken away from him by his Crucifixion, whose benefits will flow to those who associate themselves with that sacrifice. And **Aquinas** made the crucial point that, although confession has to be made and contrition shown by the sinner himself, 'satisfaction has to do with the exterior act and here one can make use of friends' (*Summa Theologiae* 3. 48. 2 ad 1), that is, one can make use of reparation provided by someone else.

I have written that God 'made available' this reparation, for clearly Christians have always claimed that Jesus's act makes no difference to us unless in some way we associate ourselves with it. We can say to God, 'Please accept instead of the life which I ought to have led (and the lives which my ancestors ought to have led) this perfect life of Jesus as my reparation'. The ceremony of entry to the Christian Church is baptism. The Nicene Creed affirms belief in '**one baptism**' (that is, a non-repeatable ceremony) '**for the forgiveness of sins**'. At their baptism, wrote St Paul (in his New Testament book the Letter to the Romans 6: 3), Christians are baptized into the death of Jesus. When adults are baptized, they ask God to accept the life and death of Jesus as their reparation for sin. When children are baptized, parents or godparents do so on their behalf with the prayer that, when the children become older, they will make that request to God their own.

If Jesus was using his human life and death to make reparation for our sins, he would have needed to say that he was doing this, and to tell us how we can associate ourselves with his act; and God the Father would need to signify in some way afterwards that he had accepted that life and death for this purpose.

Although, I claimed in Chapter 3, God has an obligation to become incarnate in order to identify with our suffering, he surely had no obligation to live a perfect life and make this life available as an atonement for our sins. No wronged person has any obligation to help the wrongdoer atone for their wrongdoing. If I steal your money, you have no obligation to me to help me cope with the consequences. But it might be generous of you to do so. So, although not obligatory, would it be the unique best action for God to do, to live a perfect human life and make it available for this purpose? One alternative is that God could simply have forgiven us in response to some minimum amount of repentance and apology. Most theologians agree on that. But they also point out that there is much good in God taking our wrongdoing so seriously as to insist on some reparation. When serious wrong has been done, parents and courts rightly insist on the wrongdoer providing some minimum amount of reparation. It involves the wrongdoer taking what he has done seriously. Another alternative would be for God to show solidarity with our suffering by showing us how to cope with it, and then insist on our making considerable reparation ourselves (by living perfectly with much suffering for many years after we realize the need to make reparation), and then forgiving us only if we do. That insistence would make the obtaining of divine forgiveness very difficult indeed for most of us, although it would make us take our sins even more seriously. Perhaps we should say only that for God to make available an incarnate perfect human life (likely to end in death by execution) to provide atonement to those who associate themselves with it was at least an equal best act. It is the sort of thing we may well expect God to do; and a priori I suggest it is at least as probable as not that God would do this.

5   GOD TEACHES US HOW TO LIVE

Humans need help not merely in dealing with their past wrongdoing (which I discussed in the previous chapter) but in living good lives in the present. We need more information about how it is good to live, and we need help to live in that way.

We need more information about what **God** is like and what he has done for us of the kind set out in previous chapters, for this has consequences for how we should behave towards God. Even if humans easily recognized the force of arguments for the existence of God, it would help them (and especially the less sophisticated among them) if they were told that there is a God by an apparently reliable source of information. We need to know more about what God is like (for example, that he is a Trinity) and how he has acted towards us (for example, that he became incarnate to share our human condition), in order that we may worship him better for what he is and has done, and interact with him better. Although, I believe, my a priori arguments for the doctrines that if there is a God, God is a Trinity, and that God would become incarnate in order to share the human condition, are valid, not all humans may be fully convinced by them. And even if humans believe that God has become incarnate to provide atonement for our wrongdoing, they still need to know when and as which human he became incarnate and how they ought to appropriate that atonement for themselves (e.g. by seeking baptism); and no a priori argument can show all that. It is an obvious general fact about humans that we would be ignorant of these things unless we were taught them by some person (perhaps by God Incarnate himself) who comes to us with credentials (public evidence) that he has been sent by God to teach us about these matters. This would provide a 'propositional revelation', a revelation from God that certain propositions (e.g. 'God became incarnate in Jesus Christ') are true.

The Need for Moral Knowledge

We also need better knowledge of which kinds of behaviour towards our fellow humans are supererogatorily good, obligatory, or wrong.

We acquire a sense of morality by being told that such and such actions are obligatory or supererogatorily good beyond obligation, and our parents or teachers praising us for doing the latter and rebuking us when we fail to do the former; and that certain other actions are wrong, and our parents rebuking us for doing them. As with all fundamental concepts, be it 'cause' or 'believe' or 'deduce', we need to be shown or have described to us many examples of the correct application of moral concepts as well as their logical relations to other concepts (e.g. their relations to praise or blame) before we can grasp the concepts. The standard examples of the 'morally obligatory' (or whatever) by which we are introduced to moral concepts will fall into describable kinds: keeping promises, not telling lies, feeding our children, caring for our parents, etc. We may be told that keeping promises and not telling lies are morally obligatory, that talking to the lonely or feeding the hungry are morally good actions, and that stealing is morally wrong. Or we may be introduced to these concepts by many similar but some different kinds of examples. We may be told that stealing from the wealthy is not wrong, but that it is obligatory always to obey your teachers.

Once we have in this way grasped the concept of the 'morally obligatory', we can come to recognize that some of the examples by which we have been introduced to it are rather different from the others, and while a rebuke is an appropriate response to the failure to perform the latter, it is not an appropriate response to failure to perform the former. We might be told that fighting a duel to defend one's honour is morally obligatory. But we may come to derive through reflection on many other possible situations a general principle that someone's life is a very valuable thing—so valuable that it should only be taken from them to save a life which they are threatening to destroy or perhaps in reparation for a life which they have taken away. So we may conclude that no one should ever try to kill anyone except to prevent them from killing someone else or perhaps as a punishment for killing someone else. We may then infer that, while it is not appropriate to rebuke someone who kills in a war in order to save the lives of his fellow soldiers, it is appropriate to rebuke someone for fighting a duel to defend their honour; and so that, although we were originally told that fighting a duel to defend one's honour is obligatory, in fact it is wrong. And we may come to experience for ourselves what it is like to suffer or benefit from actions of some kind (e.g. racial abuse). That may lead us to judge that, although we were originally told that actions of that kind are not wrong, in fact (as we did not previously realize) they have features which make them very similar to other actions which we recognize as wrong—for example, that such actions humiliate their victims. So reflection and experience can lead each of us and (over the centuries) the whole human race to improve our grasp of what are the most general truths of morality. But if we were not introduced to moral concepts by somewhat the same kinds of examples of the morally good, obligatory, and wrong, we would not already agree so much about which actions are good, or be able to make progress in reaching greater agreement—as we often can.

Most Christians, Hindus, and atheists alike are introduced to this **common concept of morality** by being shown many of the same kinds of examples. There are, of course, important differences between such groups about the morality of various kinds of actions, but the fact of a substantial amount of agreement allows us to make progress in resolving differences by reasoning with each other and getting each other to understand what it is like to have certain experiences. In this way we try to discover very general moral truths which are involved in our shared concept of morality, truths which are not created by the will of God. I will call such truths **necessary moral truths**.

But although we can find out most such necessary truths for ourselves by reflection on the very nature of the concept of morality, we have a natural bias (part of our original sinfulness) towards concealing these things from ourselves; and our parents and teachers and neighbours have often given us (by their instruction and example) false moral teaching (saying, for example, that killing people doesn't matter if they are Jews). We need to be reminded of these necessary moral truths, and **we need to be told how they apply** in detail. For example, we may recognize that (with the possible exceptions considered above) it is wrong to kill people, but need to be told whether a foetus or an old man in a coma is or is not a person in order to know whether abortion or allowing those in a coma to die is or is not killing. We may recognize that lying is normally wrong, but need to know whether it is wrong if we can save a life by telling a lie. And on some issues most of us are just not morally sensitive enough to work out what is good or bad, obligatory or wrong. Is helping the depressed to commit suicide always or only sometimes wrong? Is there a best form of government (e.g. democracy)? Does the state have a duty to educate children if parents do not do so; and how bad does the abuse have to be before the state has the right to intervene when parents abuse their children? It is an obvious general fact about humans that many of us simply do not know the answers to these questions (as is evident from the fact that there are such large disagreements about them). God may well have hoped that, when the first humans became aware of moral issues, we would have done a lot better than we have at working out for ourselves what is obligatory and what is wrong. But having failed to do so, we need some help.

Further, as I noted in Chapter 1, in virtue of being our creator, who keeps us in being from moment to moment and gives us so many good things, **God has** (within limits) **the right to impose further obligations** on us—as (within much narrower limits) parents have the right to impose obligations on children and the state has the right to impose obligations on its citizens; and so make acts which otherwise might be merely supererogatorily good or morally indifferent (neither good nor wrong) into obligations. Such obligations created by a command from an authority who has the right to issue it are contingent moral truths. (They are contingent on the command having been issued.) Even if it is not otherwise obligatory to care for the poor in distant lands, God could make it our duty and thus oblige us to live better lives than we would live otherwise. And there are more specific matters, for example, matters concerned with sex or the sanctity of life, about which God might impose obligations which are more demanding than the very general necessary truths of morality. And God could tell certain people or kinds of people or communities to do certain jobs for him; he could call particular people to serve him as missionaries or as monks and nuns, or give women certain duties and men other duties. Why would God burden us with more stringent obligations than are involved in the necessary truths of morality?

For reasons of two kinds. The first kind of reason **[A]** is **to ensure coordination of good actions.** A family or church or state has various obligations: to educate children or to preach the Gospel or to preserve law and order. But someone must decide how the obligation is to be fulfilled: which school the children should attend; and who should lead the church in its task of interpreting the Gospel or determining which missionaries should go to which country. So God has a reason for setting up a mechanism to enable us to reach collective decisions; e.g. by telling us which of husband and wife should make the final decision about which school their children should attend (when they cannot agree about which school would be best for the children), or how Church leaders should be chosen and how much authority they have.

The second kind of reason **[B]** is **to get us to do actions** which it is good for us to do and **which forward God's purposes in an important way,** but which without a command of God would be good but not obligatory. When their children are young, parents often command them to do actions which but for the command would be supererogatory (and such commands may sometimes be backed up by offers of reward or threats of punishment). Parents may tell children to do the shopping for a sick neighbour, even though without the parent's command the children would have no obligation to do this. But parents issue such commands both because it is good for the child to help in the family task of looking after the sick neighbour, and because parents want their children to get into the habit of doing what is good beyond obligation. Commands often have more effect than good advice, but once children get into the habit of doing supererogatorily good actions, the need for commands diminishes. And if their parents also help the children to see why such actions are good, then doing them will become a habit which the children value and so want to keep. Happiness (in the sense in which I am using this word) consists in doing what you want to do. Children thus educated will find their happiness in the right ways. Likewise **God wants humans to be naturally good people**, to get much of our happiness from making other people happy. By commanding us to do good actions which otherwise would be only supererogatorily good, God makes it easier for us to do those actions, and so to get into the habit of doing such actions and so to become naturally good people. It is therefore plausible to suppose that (for reasons of kind [A] or [B]) God might reveal that he has commanded us to do various actions which otherwise would be merely supererogatorily good, and so made them obligatory.

Some of all this moral information (the information about the obligations which God has imposed on us) we cannot possibly find out for ourselves; and other parts of this moral information (those moral truths which hold independently of God's will) are such that we have found it very difficult to discover. **We need God's propositional revelation** to us to give us more moral information (about what is obligatory anyway, and about what is made obligatory by God's command). It is therefore highly probable that God will reveal to us not merely propositions about his nature and how he has acted in history, but also propositions about how we ought to behave towards each other.

If a religion claims that God has declared some action obligatory, we clearly have more reason for believing that claim to be true if we can show that it is a necessary moral truth that that action is obligatory, or if we can see a reason why God might have made the action obligatory. Since we clearly do not always know the necessary truths about which actions are morally obligatory and so need guidance from God, we do not know who should do what in order to fulfil some of our obligations; that is, which are the actions which God has a reason of kind [A] to command. And since we do not know all the necessary truths about which actions are supererogatorily good, we do not know which actions are such that God would have a reason of kind [B] to command. So we cannot expect to know God's reasons in all cases for declaring actions obligatory (or wrong). But I believe that we can in general come to see that the actions which Christianity has traditionally declared to be obligatory (or wrong) either are necessarily so, or are such that God has a reason (of kind [A] or [B]) to make them obligatory (or wrong, as the case may be). And, if I am right about this, it gives a significant prior probability to Christian claims that God has revealed such truths. So how probable a priori are Christian claims about which propositions of morality God has revealed?

The Revelation to Ancient Israel

Christianity holds, as do Judaism and Islam, that God adopted one particular pre-Christian community, ancient Israel, and guided their history, providing them with a limited revelation. The Creed acknowledges this by the claim that **God** (the Holy Spirit) '**spoke through the prophets**', the prophets being those who taught ancient Israel about God. (Exactly what this phrase involves with respect to how much of the Old Testament is supposed to be true is a topic which I shall investigate in Chapter ii.) But given that God has the nature described in Chapter i, it is clearly the case that ancient Israel had a better understanding of that nature than any other ancient people. They believed that they should worship only one God, who loved Israel; and in due course they came to believe that there was only one God, whom everyone should worship, who could do anything and knew almost everything. And, as I shall illustrate shortly, they had a very considerable understanding of moral truths. If there is a God, then it was he who arranged this, either by making the laws of nature and initial conditions of the universe such that such a people would evolve, or by interfering in natural processes to reveal truths to Israel. Why should God reveal himself specially to one nation? In the later pre-Christian period many Israelites came to see the answer to that: God wanted the Israelites to tell the world about himself. It is a great good for one nation to have the task of converting others; and clearly not all nations can have that task.

Christian moral teaching has its basis in the '**Ten Commandments**', which the Old Testament books of Exodus and Deuteronomy claim that God gave to Israel. These are the commands (1) to worship God and only God, (2) not to worship any idol (made, for example, of stone or wood), (3) not to 'make wrongful use of the name of God' (e.g. cursing him or calling on him to witness a promise which you have no intention of keeping), (4) to 'keep holy the sabbath day' (i.e. to worship and not to work on Saturdays), (5) to honour your father and mother, (6) not to murder, (7) not to commit adultery, (8) not to steal, (9) not to make a false accusation against someone in a court of law, and (10) not to 'covet' (try to get) any of someone else's possessions.

It is fairly obvious that (5) to (10) are all necessary truths. (5) is a consequence of the obligation to reverence and please our benefactors. People have a range of possessions which belong to them; exactly how large this is is often unclear, but clearly people often have a right to their house, clothes, and source of income; and (10) (which entails (8)) claims that no one has the right to try to take these things away from anyone. Above all, no one has the right to try to take away someone else's life (except perhaps in the course of a just war, or as a punishment for murder). Hence (6). To cause someone to be punished for an act they did not commit is an obvious injustice to them. Hence (9). Adultery is sexual intercourse between two persons at least one of whom is married to someone else; getting married involves the spouses promising to be faithful to each other. Hence adultery involves breaking (or helping someone else to break) a solemn promise. Hence (7). Given that there is a God, the obligation to reverence and please our benefactors entails the obligation to reverence and please God. Hence (1) and (3). To worship any other god would be to worship someone who was not in this kind of way our benefactor, and so to insult our true benefactor. Hence (2).

(4), however, the command to observe the sabbath, is clearly not a necessary truth. While, as the first commandment claims, all humans have a duty to worship God, Israel, as a special community given unique knowledge about him and chosen to do his work, plausibly had a duty to recognize that fact in their worship by worshipping him collectively. But in order for this to happen, God has to tell Israel how to do this, or to tell Israel who should decide how to do this. So God had a coordination reason (a reason of kind [A]) for choosing one day when Israelites should worship together; and he chose, the Old Testament claims, Saturday. The Christian Church subsequently taught that God had replaced the Saturday obligation with an obligation to observe Sunday in commemoration of the Resurrection of Jesus, which, it claimed, happened on a Sunday and was God's supreme act of intervention in history. And again God had the coordination reason for selecting a unique day for communal worship. Without (what they believed to be) God's command Christians might have thought it better to continue to observe the sabbath, or to celebrate the Resurrection monthly or annually instead.

Commandments (5) to (10) form much of the foundation for the obligations which humans have to each other in their personal relations; and commandments (1) to (3) form much of the foundation for human obligations to God—all necessary moral truths or (given that there is a God) derivable from necessary moral truths. The Old Testament also contains much regulation about animal sacrifice and ritual, and about political organization, procedures of law, and punishment; but even if God did command these things to ancient Israel, the Christian Church taught that all this no longer applied.

Christian Moral Teaching

The core new element of Christian moral teaching, deriving directly from the teaching of Jesus recorded in the Gospels and universally agreed by all Christians as central to Christianity, is that we should show love to God and to other humans in ways **far more extensive** than those contained in the Ten Commandments or elsewhere in the Old Testament. Indeed God commends us to live a perfect life. While it is not obvious exactly which of the actions which Christian moral teaching encourages are supposed to be commanded by God, and so to be obligatory, and which are merely commended, and so remain supererogatory, Jesus and his Church clearly taught that many actions previously supererogatory were now obligatory. We should worship and pray much, for that will make us aware of God, who wants us to learn from his omniscience, be sensitive to his perfect goodness, and ask him to use his omnipotence. He wants us to be his friend and a friend of those whom he has created. So we should feed the hungry, care for the sick, visit the imprisoned, show hospitality to the lonely, accommodate the homeless, educate the uneducated; or—if we cannot do some of these things ourselves—we should at least give money to enable others to do them. And we should be prepared to do these things at the expense of our own well-being. We should teach others about God and what he has done for us, and help them to become good people. And we must forgive those who seek our forgiveness for having wronged us. God has abundant reason of kind [B] to command us to do these things. In this way he seeks to make us good people who come to get much of our happiness through interaction with God himself and with other creatures whom we help to make happy and whom we help to get their happiness in right ways.

While it is obvious that the acts mentioned in the last paragraph are good and so acts which God has reason to make obligatory, Christian tradition has taught that there are certain **further specific actions** which are wrong, mainly actions concerned with sexual conduct (e.g. sexual intercourse outside marriage), family stability (e.g. divorce), and the preservation of life (e.g. abortion and euthanasia). There is no list of such actions drawn up by any Church council similar to the Nicene Creed's theological definitions, but the Christian view on some of these matters was so generally agreed throughout Christian history until the last century that to deny the normal position would probably have been regarded as heretical. Yet for some of these actions it is clearly not a necessary truth that they are wrong, and it is sometimes not obvious that God would have any reason to forbid them.

Since the primary focus of this book is on the theological doctrines of Christianity rather than on the moral doctrines which depend on them, and since the very general moral principles described earlier are clearly more important than their filling-out by way of detailed obligations, I must be very brief in discussing the latter. I can only illustrate with one or two examples how the argument might go, showing that some of these obligations are such as God would have had reasons of kind [A] or [B] to impose. This should illustrate the kind of reasons which he might have for imposing others of the obligations which Christianity claims that he has imposed.

While, I pointed out earlier, it is a necessary moral truth that adultery is wrong, traditional Christianity also teaches that **sexual intercourse outside marriage** and **divorce** (or at least divorce from a faithful spouse), are also wrong. Both of these prohibitions presuppose an understanding of marriage as lifelong; those getting married commit themselves to lifelong loyalty. So the prohibition on sexual intercourse outside marriage is a prohibition on sexual intercourse outside a marriage of that sort; and the prohibition on divorce is a prohibition of divorce from a marriage in which the spouses have committed themselves to lifelong loyalty. I suggest that our normal moral understanding can see that the ideal family (marriage with children when it works well, that is) is a good thing. It is obviously good for anyone to have a partner who loves them and whom they love, when both of them regard loyalty and support of the other as a primary lifelong obligation; and who cooperate in begetting, nurturing, and educating children in the right way. I suggest that, if it were the general custom in society to confine sexual intercourse to lifelong marriage, that would make it a lot easier for families to approach the ideal.

If sexual intercourse is confined to intercourse within marriage, that will make the intimacy of marriage special and so make husband and wife unique partners for each other. Someone who has saved the satisfaction of sexual desire for a spouse will be able to regard and be regarded by that spouse as uniquely their own. And it is plausible to suppose that, if people get used to having casual sex before marriage, it becomes more natural to commit adultery when the marriage becomes difficult or boring; and it is also highly plausible to suppose that the example of many people abstaining from sexual intercourse before marriage will influence others to take their marriages more seriously.

The prohibition of divorce is obviously a considerable burden on those whose marriages seem to have broken down. Why should God make divorce difficult or impossible—say, for a wife to divorce a cruel (though not unfaithful) husband? These instructions have never been seen as forbidding a temporary separation in such circumstances, but why should not the wife marry again? An apparent breakdown of marriage may be repairable. But that is much more likely to happen if the spouses regard themselves as bound by their original commitment never to give up attempting to overcome difficulties in the marriage. And even if all the attempts of some couples to make their marriages work fail, the persistence of these couples in this task will encourage other couples to try harder to make their marriages work; and these other couples may succeed in this task. And further, if separated spouses do not remarry, that will bring home to others considering marriage the seriousness of the marriage commitment and deter them from entering into marriage too lightly.

It would be (but for a divine command) a supererogatory act for one person to abstain from sexual intercourse outside marriage or not to divorce a spouse merely for the sake of contributing in a very small way towards creating a climate of practice which will strengthen marriage. But it provides a reason (of kind [B]) why God seeking the perfect goodness of a couple considering intercourse outside marriage or divorce, and the good of others beyond the couple, might make it obligatory for the couple to do what would otherwise be only supererogatory. In these cases God commands some of us to do something for the benefit of others. He therefore issues these commands for the same reason as he tells us to feed the hungry or to talk to the lonely. For him to command these things is an act of love towards us because he is helping us to become very good people who get much of our happiness out of making others happy. The argument which I have given is not designed to show that necessarily God would forbid certain actions, only that it is plausible (not too improbable) that he would do so; and so any historical evidence (of a kind to be considered in Part II) that this moral teaching is part of a revelation from God will be 'topped-up' by the argument that this is the kind of moral teaching which a perfectly good God might be expected to give.

Note, however, that if God issues a command to some ancient society, he might mean it to apply to all societies or only to that ancient society; and if the only reason of which we can think why God might have issued some command is one which would only be relevant in the circumstances of that ancient society, that is some reason to take any historical evidence that God had issued that command as evidence that it was a command meant only for that society. Jews of Old Testament times and the Christian Church for its first 1,300 years taught (as Islam still teaches) that usury, that is, lending money to someone on condition of receiving it back with interest, is wrong. But the societies to which that teaching was addressed were ones in which it was mainly the rich who lent money to the poor at a high rate of interest; when someone could not feed their family, they borrowed money from a rich man. God has very good reason to tell people of such societies not to receive interest on money: it would be very cruel for the rich individuals to demand interest from the poor. Yet in our modern commercial society it is often people of modest income who lend money to financial institutions which earn a lot of money for their shareholders, some of whom are very rich, by the use to which they put the borrowed money. Ancient societies did not have financial institutions of the modern kind. It is not a necessary truth of morality that people have an obligation not to receive interest on money which they lend to financial institutions, and God surely has no reason for imposing such an obligation; although surely he still has very good reason to forbid lending to poor people at high rates of interest. The reasons which I have suggested that God might have for forbidding sexual intercourse outside marriage or divorce (at any rate from a faithful spouse) are, if valid, reasons which apply as much today as in ancient societies; and so this qualification does not concern the plausibility of such actions being wrong today.

There is **no reason to expect** that God would provide for us **a total moral code**. Although, I claimed in Chapter 1, God gives us freedom of choice in order to allow us to exercise deep responsibility for ourselves and each other, this is compatible with him sometimes helping us to form right choices when we fail to do so. But we must not expect him to take away our freedom of choice in any respect, including in the respect of choosing whether or not to try to find out for ourselves (and to help each other to find out) what is obligatory and what is wrong. We might therefore expect him to give us more moral information than we have been able to discover for ourselves, but not perhaps so much as to deprive us of the possibility of choosing whether or not to work out the more detailed consequences for our lives of what he has told us. And there are certainly plenty of detailed moral issues about which there is no one traditional Christian view.

Revelation by Example and Needing an Interpreting Church

God could certainly provide propositional revelation in words without himself becoming incarnate, and other religions (e.g. Islam) claim that this has happened. It is, however, I argued earlier, necessary if we are to understand such fundamental moral concepts as 'good' and 'obligation' that we should be shown, or at least have described to us, examples of 'good' actions and 'obligations' by means of which we can then recognize other examples of these. A perfectly good life would include many supererogatory good actions. And because humans do not do such actions as often as they fulfil their obligations, we shall have many fewer examples of supererogatory actions; and we may well expect that there may be supererogatory actions of kinds which we have never considered. Even if we knew all the kinds of supererogatory good action which there are, we are unlikely to have any examples of how to weave such actions together to make a perfect life. It would be a lot easier to understand how to live a perfectly good life if we have an example of someone doing this. And although God perhaps does not command us to live a perfect life, the life he does command us to live may, I argued, be expected to include many actions of kinds which, but for his command, would be merely supererogatory. And it would also provide great encouragement to try to live a perfect or near-perfect life if we are shown that it can be done. So **God has good reason** not merely to provide us with revealed teaching on how to live, but **to show us how to live and to encourage us to live in that way** by himself becoming incarnate.

To be easily comprehensible in some society, it is often best if **teaching** is **expressed within the presuppositions of** that **society**. For example, if a society thinks that the world consists of two parts, the Earth and the Dome of the Sky which covers it, then it will understand the doctrine of creation most easily if you tell it that God made the Earth and its Dome. But of course we believe that the world consists not of the Earth and its Dome, but of stars and planets. And maybe it consists also of a lot of other things about which we do not know. So why not convey the doctrine of creation by saying 'God created everything'? But even that is not quite correct. He did not create himself. And does 'everything' include numbers and the truths of arithmetic? Surely $2 + 2 = 4$, whether or not there is a God. It must be possible to teach the essence of the doctrine of creation to relatively simple people without having to solve all these philosophical questions in the process. But that means teaching it in a way that takes for granted the presuppositions of the society about what exists, apart from God, and saying that that (for example) the Earth and its Dome is what God created.

Even if teaching in one culture is not expressed in terms of false presuppositions, it may be expressed in ways that do not provide answers to questions which worry a different culture which has different concepts and lives in different circumstances; and so **teaching may need to be re-expressed for a different culture in a different way**. Jesus, I shall be arguing in a later chapter, taught that he was divine; but he also distinguished himself as 'the Son' from 'the Father' and 'the Holy Spirit'. But did this mean that Jesus was not human; or that there were three gods and not just one god? Various other parts of Jesus's teaching and the accounts of Christian doctrine in other New Testament books suggest that Jesus was human, and that there was only one God. First-century Jews did not have the precise philosophical concepts which would enable them to give a consistent account of the doctrines that Jesus was both divine and human, and that God is a Trinity. It needed the Greek philosophy familiar to the learned thinkers of the fourth- and fifth-century wider Mediterranean world to provide such concepts as 'substance', 'individual', and 'nature' in terms of which the doctrines of the Incarnation and the Trinity could be spelled out in the more evidently consistent ways which I have set out in Chapters 2 and 3.

But the doctrinal formulas of the fourth and fifth centuries left questions yet to be resolved, such as the issue of whether God is everlasting or timeless, whether he has thisness, and whether he exists of logical necessity. No creed or larger book understood by people of only a moderately intellectually sophisticated society (or, in my view, by people of any society at all) could possibly deal adequately with the questions and answer the objections to its teaching which might be raised in the context of any yet more sophisticated society.

A similar point arises with respect to the revelation of teaching about the morality of different kinds of ordinary human moral conduct. To be comprehensible to ordinary people in a particular society, **moral teaching must be immediately relevant** to their concerns. So God had a reason to forbid the Jews from practising usury without putting this prohibition in the form of a book-length treatise on when, if at all, usury would be permissible. So whether and when usury is permissible in a modern society is a matter on which people today need guidance.

We Need a Church

For these reasons any revelation needs an interpreting body, **a Church**, which can draw out its consequences for new cultures in new circumstances. No doubt it is good that Church members should try to work out for themselves the consequences of the original revelation. But if the revelation is to be available to future generations and cultures, **God must ensure that** in the end, perhaps after much controversy, **the correct interpretation** of the original revelation **emerges**. The Church must have divine guidance. The Nicene Creed claims that God has provided '**one holy catholic and Apostolic Church**'. (In this context 'catholic' means 'universal',

and 'Apostolic' means 'deriving from the Church of the Apostles'.)
I have argued that, if there is a God, he must become incarnate
in order to share our human life and he must tell us that he has
done this. Without a Church, it would gradually become obscure
whether and in what way God had become incarnate. And I have
argued that it is quite probable that God Incarnate would provide
atonement for our sins and reveal to us theological and moral
truths. Without a Church to make his work available (for example,
by providing baptism and the eucharist) and interpret his teaching
for new generations and cultures, all that too would be lost. That is
especially evident with respect to moral teaching. Not merely are
most of us not clever enough to work out for ourselves whether and
how some divine command applies today, but we are all subject to
great temptation to interpret rules in our own preferred way. Even
if I am right in supposing that lending money on interest under
certain conditions is permissible in today's society, people need
guidance about this from an authority; and virtually all Christian
bodies today accept the view about usury that I have advocated.

I pointed out in Chapter 1 that it is because we humans are
subject to irrational desires to do what is wrong that we have the
possibility of choosing between good and wrong. But humans are
so made that, each time we choose (despite such desires) to do a
good action of some kind, it becomes a little easier to do a good
action of that kind next time; and each time we allow ourselves to
do a wrong action of some kind, it becomes a little more difficult to
do a good action of that kind next time. Gradually by our actions
we strengthen or weaken desires of different kinds, and thereby
we form our characters. God, being perfectly good, wants us to
become naturally good people, saints. Since most humans have so
obviously failed to become saints, we might well expect God to
provide help for us in this process of sanctification.

Since humans need each other and are much influenced by each
other, and since it is good that we should be responsible for each
other, an obvious further task for a Church (additional to being
a source of revealed truth) is as a society in which those who
seek atonement for the past, and to learn what is the good way
to live in the present, also help each other to form a naturally
good character—**help each other to become saints**. The Church
should be a community of encouragement, but just because the
Church is meant for those who are seeking to be made perfect, it

will consist of some very imperfect members who may fail to live up to its teaching in many ways; and because Church leaders will be among those imperfect members, individual parts of the Church may from time to time fail to provide very much help.

Conclusion

I have argued in this chapter that we might well expect God to give us a propositional revelation both about the matters considered in Chapters 2, 3, and 4, and about moral truths (both necessary truths which we have proved unable to discover for ourselves, and contingent truths in the form of obligations which God is imposing on us for the good of others and of ourselves). I have argued that the central moral claims of the Christian tradition and one or two less central claims are either necessary truths or are such as God would have reason to impose on us. I have given a third reason (additional to the reasons of sharing our suffering and making atonement for our wrongdoing) why God might choose to become incarnate—that is, to show us by example how we should live, and thereby to encourage us to do so. In doing so he might be expected himself to give us the propositional revelation at the same time. And I have claimed that God must provide a Church at least in order to interpret his revelation, and probably also in order to encourage us to become saints.

6 GOD OFFERS US HEAVEN

The End of the World

I claimed earlier that the creation of humans with their great potentiality to do evil as well as good and their great liability to suffer evil as well as good was a mixed blessing; God had perhaps as much reason to bring it about as not to bring it about. Maybe instead he should have created people who were naturally good and so had no real responsibility for each other or choice of the kind of people they were to be (and perhaps God has created such people in another world). Creating humans was taking a great risk; and so, in the light of all the evil as well as the good that humans have done, God has as much reason as not to bring this risky experiment to an end. In expressing the belief that God the Son '**will come again in glory to judge the living and the dead**' the Creed affirms a belief that, sooner or later, this world order will come to an end.

The Afterlife of the Firmly Good

A good God would surely want to give all humans an enormously good life after death. It is of course good that we should do good acts on earth for their own sake; it is good to feed the hungry just because they are hungry, and—given that there is a God—good to worship God just because he is our supreme benefactor. But it is also good to become a naturally good person, one who does good acts spontaneously. A naturally good person will want to reverence what is good and holy, and express gratitude to his or her benefactors; they will want to grow in understanding of deep truths, and in admiration of beauty (of poetry, art, music, or nature) and to cooperate in helping other people to do the same. God will want us to be like that and to be very happy being like that (because we want to be like that). And, like a good parent, God will want to interact with us in our pursuit of these good things—for ever. But on this earth we are subject to temptations to seek other less important goals; and there are obstacles in our way which prevent us from attaining these goals. Prayer to God may seem never to make contact with him; our fellow Church members may be unfriendly; we may not have enough time or money to help the lonely and disabled very much; and so on. In outlining my theodicy in Chapter 1, I have given reasons why God might make things difficult for us in such ways for the period of our earthly life, and in particular the reason that thereby he allows us to form our own characters. But these reasons are reasons which apply only for such a relatively short period while God allows this process to take place.

If we have formed our characters for good, God would surely want us to have the everlasting happiness which consists in us enjoying for ever the activities which I have just listed without the obstacles which prevent us from enjoying them on earth. Having this happiness is what being in **Heaven** would amount to. The saints would enjoy joining in cooperative worship of God, and would never be bored in acquiring knowledge of ever new facets of God's infinite knowledge, and in helping others on earth (and perhaps elsewhere) to choose to be the kind of persons who would be happy in this kingdom of Heaven. In Christian tradition the saints are pictured as providing this help by interceding with God on our behalf. As well as praying directly to God himself, many Christians pray to a saint (for example, to Mary, the Mother of Jesus) and ask her to pray to God on our behalf. Maybe the saints would assist in this divine work also in many other ways.

Those who enjoy Heaven will do naturally not merely what they believe to be good, but what is in fact good. Yet many people on earth who have sought to do good actions, and so formed strong inclinations to do what they believe to be good, may in some respects still be ignorant of which actions are good. Because they are strongly inclined to do good, God would surely want to take them to Heaven too. But first they would need to learn after death which actions are good (and so, for example, how they ought to worship God and seek forgiveness from him). Then in virtue of their inclination to do what they believe to be good, which they have developed during their lives, they would come to do the actions which are in fact good. And changing your behaviour, however good your intentions, can be a bit painful.

The Afterlife of the Incorrigibly Bad

Yet just because the life of Heaven would be expected to be of the kind just described, only those who love doing actions which are good for their own sake would be happy there. Those who feed the hungry in this world merely in order themselves to have plenty to eat in the next world where they would not need to bother about the hungry would not be happy in Heaven. And while we have this opportunity on earth to make ourselves (with divine help) good people who would enjoy Heaven, we also have the opportunity to neglect this opportunity. We can allow ourselves persistently and knowingly to become bad people, people who reject the good so often that we no longer have any moral sensitivity. We would then become merely a collection of desires to do wrong actions, and in particular desires to hurt and dominate others. I argued in Chapter 1 that God has good reason to allow people to hurt others in this world, in order to give them and those others significant choices between good and evil and the opportunities to form their characters. But there is no good reason for God to allow people to go on hurting others in another world after their characters are formed. So those who have allowed themselves to become totally bad people will be a collection of unfulfilled desires, and that will inevitably be an unhappy state, which would constitute living in **Hell**.

God could, of course, give them new good desires, but that would involve imposing on them a character which they had persistently and knowingly chosen not to have. So perhaps God would eliminate such people if that is what they wanted. But if he is to respect humans as people, if he gives them a choice of character, he must respect that choice and permit them permanently to reject him and all that he stands for. Otherwise in creating humans God would be like a puppet master who ensures that in the end every human does what he (God) wants, and has no ultimate freedom to determine the sort of person they are to be.

The Afterlife of Those of Unformed Character

As we get older, we gradually form our characters for good and ill, and—I have suggested—God would allow us to be the sort of people we have chosen to be. But many people die young, when they have only partly but not fully formed their character; and some die very young, before they are even sensitive to good and bad. How would a good God deal with such people? He could perhaps put them into another world with such propensities for good or ill as they have formed, and let them complete there the task of character formation. Or perhaps he would give them or many of them the benefit of the doubt and assume that they would prefer to be firmly good rather than incorrigibly bad people. I have suggested earlier that God might create creatures who have an already fixed good character; and so he might give such a character to those of unformed character who have not firmly rejected the good (although that would, of course, have the disadvantage of depriving them of the choice of the sort of person they are to be). And he might do the same for those (e.g. babies) who are in no way yet sensitive to good and bad. Alternatively he might give them a good afterlife but one suitable for those ignorant of the possibility of moral sanctity and so not the life of Heaven as I have described it. There are thus various possible futures which a good God might give to those of unformed character.

Knowledge of God's Plans

We may well expect that at least some of God's plans for our future would be part of what he reveals to us. If we learn of his plan to take to Heaven those who make themselves good people, that will show us something further important about God and thus enable us to interact with him better. The hope of Heaven and the risk of Hell would also provide us with encouragement to do good. Parents often offer rewards to children for doing good acts (both ones which they ought to do anyway and those which are supererogatory) and threaten to punish those who do what they ought not to do. Parents do this in the early stages of moral education in the hope that, after their children have got in the habit of doing good partly as a result of seeking rewards and avoiding punishments, they will then come to do good actions and avoid bad actions for the reason that will already have influenced them to some extent, that good is good and bad is bad. God might well be expected to treat us in the same way. But God might be expected not to make it too obvious at first that there is a Heaven and a Hell. One reason for that is in order that we may have some motivation to do the good for its own sake. Another reason is the reason mentioned in the last chapter, that we may have the opportunity to try to find out such truths for ourselves and to help others to do so.

The Christian Doctrine of the Afterlife

In those respects in which Christian tradition has a clear doctrine of the afterlife, it conforms to what, I have suggested, we might expect a perfectly good God to arrange for us. In its claim that God the Son will '**judge the living and the dead**', and in its expectation of '**the resurrection of the dead and the life of the world to come**', the Creed assumes the universal Christian view that (among those who are still living when this risky experiment of creating us comes to an end, and those who are then already dead) the good will be rewarded and the bad punished. The reward is the life of Heaven, and the punishment the life of Hell. It is no part of the Creed that detailed descriptions of the 'fires' of Hell are to be understood in any literal sense; having all your desires to hurt others frustrated is quite enough to make life hellish. Nor is it part of the Creed that any particular human being or indeed any human being at all is in Hell. But Christian doctrine has firmly taught that that possible fate exists for those who are incorrigibly bad. Many of the great Christian thinkers, including both Augustine and Aquinas, allowed that non-Christians can attain Heaven; and this was recognized as official Roman Catholic doctrine by the second Vatican Council (1963–6). Most Christians hold that although this 'last judgement' will finally settle the fate of all humans, many of those now already dead already enjoy Heaven or Hell. Some of the dead, however, may still be 'on the way'; for example, Roman Catholics hold that many of the dead whom God deems to have a sufficiently good character to get them eventually to Heaven need further purifying in 'Purgatory'. Christians have always believed that baptized babies go straight to Heaven (and that would be in line with my suggestion that God might impose a good character on those who had not had the opportunity to form one). But Christians have had no clear doctrine about the fate of unbaptized babies. There was a view widespread in Western Christendom in the Middle Ages that they would go to 'Limbo', where they would have a good afterlife suitable for those who never had any moral awareness (and I suggested this as one possibility for them). But there is no clear Christian view about the fate of those (baptized or not) whose characters are partly but not fully formed.

In Chapter 4 I expounded one version of the Christian doctrine that God the Son, Jesus, provided an atonement for our wrongdoing. In Chapter 5 I expounded the doctrine that in his life Jesus revealed to us how we should live, and provided a Church to interpret that teaching and encourage us to live in the right way. In this chapter I have expounded the doctrine that if we come to have a good character God will give us the wonderful life of Heaven. Christianity thus offers us salvation from the guilt of the past and from wrongdoing in the present, in order to live a holy life for ever in the future. The Creed expresses this by its claim that God the Son became incarnate '**for us humans and for our salvation**'.

Conclusion to Part I

At the beginning of this book I made the assumption that the reader has some reason to believe that there is a God of the traditional kind: essentially omnipotent, omniscient, perfectly free and so perfectly good, and eternal. This reason might be provided by arguments of 'natural theology', or in some other way; and it might make the existence of God as probable as not, or maybe more probable or less probable than that. In Chapters 2, 3, 4, 5, and 6 I have argued that, if there is such a God, there are a priori reasons (reasons following from the very being of that God) for supposing that he has the nature (being a Trinity) which Christianity claims, and that he would act in history to do the things which Christianity claims that he has done. I claimed that necessarily God is a Trinity, and necessarily—since (for good reasons) he makes humans suffer a lot—he would take a human nature and share those sufferings, and found a Church to tell cultures and generations other than those in which he lived on earth about what he had done. I also argued that it was quite probable that he would live a perfect life and make that life available to us as a means of atonement for our sins. I argued that it was probable that he would reveal to us important moral truths, and truths about how our life after death (including Heaven, or ultimate separation from God) will depend on how we live our present life. And, of course, in so far as he does these things, he would need to ensure that the Church told us what he had done.

The Need for God's Signature

I pointed out in Chapter 5 that even if there are good arguments for the existence of God, most people would hold that they only make it to some extent probable that there is a God; and if someone has some other good reason for believing that there is a God, it is unlikely to be an overwhelmingly strong one. And even if necessarily God is a Trinity and will become incarnate, not everyone can see this. And in any case mere a priori reasoning cannot show when and where he would become incarnate; and we need to know the details of his life if our belief in his solidarity with us in our suffering is to be a powerful belief and if we are to offer his life as an atoning sacrifice. And even if a priori reasoning can show that in becoming incarnate God will reveal moral truths, it cannot show in detail what those moral truths will be. So we need historical evidence that one and only one human prophet did and said and suffered things of the kind which, I have argued, we might expect God Incarnate to say and do and suffer.

It follows from my arguments in Part I that, if there is a God, there will appear on earth a human prophet who satisfies certain **requirements**. He will live a life in which there is much suffering, claim to be God Incarnate, and found a Church to tell humans about this. It is quite probable that the prophet's life will be a perfect life and that he will claim to be making atonement for our sins, and provide plausible teaching (as a revelation from God) about morality, the nature of God, and God's plans for our future; and that, in so far as he does this, the Church will continue his work (including interpreting his revelation in plausible ways). That purported revelation will, of course, include claims that we could not discover for ourselves—for the main point of a revelation is to tell us things which we could not discover for ourselves. But what the prophet claims to reveal (and the way in which the resulting Church interprets that revelation) must be not very improbable in the light of other things which we believe to be probably true—a prophet who tells his followers to indulge in rape and pillage cannot be God Incarnate. I shall call 'not being very improbable' being '**plausible**'. I shall be arguing in Part II that there is good evidence that Jesus was a prophet who satisfied all the above requirements and that he was the only prophet in human history to do so.

Even so, maybe it was merely by chance that once in human history there was a prophet about whom there is good evidence that he satisfied all these requirements. We need more evidence that God was responsible for the prophet doing and saying what he does. We need evidence of God's 'signature' on the prophet's work. I understand by a **signature** an effect which can be brought about readily only by one person (or by someone else acting with his permission), and one which is recognized as a mark of endorsement by that person in the culture in which it occurred. A person's name handwritten by him or herself at the end of a document constitutes in our culture such a mark of endorsement; in medieval times the imprint of a signet ring often served this function. Cultures vary in respect of which effects of this kind they recognize as marks of endorsement.

One kind of effect which can be brought about by God alone is a **violation of laws of nature**. (While, if there is a God, all events occur only because God allows them to occur, he normally does this by keeping the laws of nature operative, not by interfering in their operation.) Laws of nature are those laws of physics or chemistry or other sciences which determine how physical objects must behave, or laws which make it immensely probable how they must behave. The former are deterministic laws; the latter are probabilistic laws. If Newton's law of gravity is a fundamental deterministic law (that is, not a consequence of a more fundamental law), and nothing more ultimate makes it operate, then physical objects must attract each other in the way in which Newton's law states. But if there is a God, all laws of nature operate only as long as God determines that they shall, and he can set them aside whenever he chooses. A once-off exception to a deterministic law of nature is a violation of a law of nature; and I shall call such an event a '**miracle**' if it is brought about by the action or permission of God. It may be, however, that the fundamental laws of nature are probabilistic; perhaps the probabilistic laws of Quantum Theory are fundamental laws of nature, as the majority of physicists believe. If so, then fundamental laws determine only that each very small fundamental particle (for example, each electron or proton) has a high probability of doing this or that, but may still do something else. Normally such indeterminism on the small scale levels out on the larger scale, so that, although there may be only a 90 per cent probability that a given electron in a stream of electrons will move along a certain path, it is virtually certain that most of the electrons in the stream will move along that path. But if something immensely improbable (given the fundamental laws of nature), an event of a kind which it is immensely improbable will happen even once in the history of the universe, nevertheless happens, that would be what I shall call a 'quasi-violation' of a law of nature. It is immensely improbable that such an event would ever have happened if laws of nature were the fundamental determinants of what happens. But again, if there is a God, he can set the laws of nature aside, and so bring about a **quasi-violation**; and I shall also call such a quasi-violation brought about by the action or permission of God a **miracle**. (When in future I write about 'violations' of a law of nature, I ask the reader to assume that I am writing about 'quasi-violations' as well.)

We do not know for certain what the fundamental laws of nature are: scientists may yet discover more fundamental laws underlying those which they currently believe to be fundamental. But we surely know enough about them to know that such events as levitation (someone rising into the air while praying, contrary to gravity or any other known force), water suddenly turning into wine, someone walking on water, or someone rising from the dead are violations of natural laws. (It is immensely unlikely that scientists will discover that the laws of nature are such that events of these kinds happen regularly from time to time.) If these violations are brought about by God, they are miracles. If we had good reason to suppose that there is no God, we would be right not to believe several witnesses who claim to have seen someone walking on water; we should say that either they were lying or they were themselves deceived by some trick of the light or were the victims of some delusion. But if we have some reason to suppose that there is a God (as I claimed in Chapter 1), then if several otherwise reliable witnesses claim to have seen the occurrence of a violation of laws of nature, and if the particular violation is one which God would have, as far as we can judge, some reason to bring about, then we would have a good reason to believe these witnesses.

One such reason for God to bring about a violation of laws of nature would be (since God alone could bring this about or permit it to occur) to provide his signature on the work and teaching of a prophet. To do that, the particular violation must be of a kind which the culture in which the violation occurred would recognize as God's signature. I shall argue in Chapter 8 that a violation of laws of nature which led to events predicted by the prophet and forwarded the prophet's work is the kind of violation which the Jews in the time of Jesus would recognize as God's signature on the prophet's work. Hence, I shall argue, if the **Resurrection of Jesus** occurred in anything like the way described in the New Testament, it was God's signature on the life and teaching of Jesus, and so God's guarantee that the teaching of Jesus (and the interpretations put upon it by his Church) are true—when we also take into account the other evidence that I have described or will describe. The other evidence that I have already described is any evidence which makes it to some extent probable that there is a God (such as the evidence of 'natural theology', to which I referred in Chapter 1), and the consequent a priori reasons for a view about what God is like and how he would act in history (described in Chapters 2, 3, 4,5, and 6). The other evidence that I will describe is the historical evidence about the life of Jesus and his teaching and that of his Church, and their uniqueness (to be described in Part II). And, given all this, I shall argue (provisionally in Chapter 9 and finally in Chapter 12) that the historical evidence does show that the Resurrection occurred in the way described in the New Testament and so is God's signature on Jesus and his Church.

PART II

GOD SHOWS US THAT HE LOVES US

It follows from the arguments of Part I that, if there is a God, we would find among us at some stage of history a prophet who lives a life in which there is much suffering, who would claim to be God incarnate, and would found a Church to continue to proclaim that message. It would also be quite probable that the prophet's life would be a perfect life, he would claim to be making available atonement for our sins, and give us plausible teaching (as a revelation from God) about the nature of God, how we should live our lives, and God's plans for our future; and if he did all this, the Church would give us plausible interpretations of that teaching. I now argue that we know quite a bit about Jesus, and what we know (our evidence) is such as it is quite probable that we would find if Jesus did all of these things, and very improbable that we would find if he didn't do these things. We saw in Chapter 1 from the example of the burglary that, if it is quite probable that we would find certain evidence if the hypothesis were true and much less probable that we would find it if the hypothesis were false, that increases the probability that the hypothesis is true. And if the evidence is much more to be expected if the hypothesis were true than it would be otherwise, that greatly increases the probability of the hypothesis.

Sources for the History of Jesus

By far the most important evidence about Jesus is that contained in the main books of the **New Testament**: the four Gospels, the Acts of the Apostles, and the letters claiming to have been written by St Paul. Paul was converted to Christianity about three years after the death of Jesus (and so about AD 32) and almost all scholars agree that many of the letters claiming to have been written by Paul were in fact written by him, and are the earliest New Testament books. Of **Paul's letters** which are almost certainly genuine the earliest is 1 Thessalonians, written about AD 50; then there are Galatians, 1 and

2 Corinthians, and Romans, written during the 50s; and Philippians and Philemon, written in the 60s. Colossians and 2 Thessalonians may or may not have been written by Paul, and the other letters attributed to him were almost certainly not written by him. One of these letters, the Letter to the Hebrews, although attributed to Paul in many editions of the Bible, does not even claim to have been written by him but was written by some unknown Church leader, probably in the later part of the first century. The letters are more concerned with expounding Christian teaching than with assembling evidence in its support, but they do contain a certain amount of information about the life of Jesus.

Each of the four **Gospels**, however, seeks to tell us the story of the life of Jesus, and what he taught, as well as commenting on its significance. The first three Gospels, the **'synoptic' Gospels**, are to some extent compilations of stories and bits of teaching from other sources. Matthew and Luke copied some of their material from Mark. Scholars differ about when those Gospels achieved their final form, but an average view might date Mark's Gospel at AD 70, and those of Matthew and Luke at AD 80. Luke was also the author of the **Acts of the Apostles**. Acts tells the story of the early Church and in particular the story of Paul's contribution to this; while some theologians date Acts also at about AD 80, others believe that the main material which it contains was written at a much earlier date. Exactly who Matthew, Mark, and Luke were is unclear; but it is clear that they were Christians closely associated with the Church's leadership. John's Gospel reached its finished form by perhaps about AD 90, possibly inspired by, but probably not written by, St John, one of the 'twelve' Apostles of Jesus.

Quite a bit of Paul's letters has a 'personal' character, and that, together with the considerable quantity of material contained in those letters, allows us to have a clear picture of **Paul** as a man. It is difficult to read those letters without getting the impression that he was a very honest and conscientious person. What he writes is what he believes. Although Paul had not seen Jesus during his earthly life, he interacted for two significant periods with the leading disciples who had followed Jesus during that life and he would have cross-questioned them about him. The first such period, he tells us in Galatians, was when he visited Jerusalem, three years after his conversion, and stayed for two weeks with Peter, the leader of the Church; and talked also with James, the brother of Jesus.

Over many years he interacted with many others who had known Jesus or had known well those who had known Jesus. He would in particular have learnt a lot from Barnabas, who had become a Christian in Jerusalem within a year of Jesus's death and with whom he travelled for some years on missionary journeys. So we may be confident that what he writes about the life of Jesus and the content of his teaching is what the immediate followers of Jesus claimed to have seen and heard from Jesus.

The **synoptic Gospels** too may be taken as **basically reliable sources**. Luke writes at the beginning of his Gospel that he sought to do the same as many others who 'have undertaken to set down an orderly account of the events which have been fulfilled among us, just as they were handed on to us by those who from the beginning were eyewitnesses and servants of the word' (Luke 1: 1–2). This, together with the style of Acts, indicates that **Luke** was claiming to write a basically historical work; and so he must have understood Mark's Gospel, from which he took some of his material, as a basically historical work. That provides good reason to suppose that **Matthew** understood **Mark** in the same way; and so, in using material from Mark, Matthew was also seeking to write a basically historical work. Most of the **Acts of the Apostles** reads like any other contemporary work of history, and the later parts (which contain no reports of anything miraculous) are so detailed and matter-of-fact as to have a diary-like quality to them. In a number of passages describing Paul's travels, Luke writes that 'we' did this or that. Paul's letters describe events also described in Acts and in the Gospels (especially the Last Supper, the Crucifixion, and—see Chapter 8—the Resurrection). There is general agreement between the synoptic Gospels about the main events of the life of Jesus. (Matthew and Luke have independent sources for some of the main events, in addition to Mark's Gospel.) The four Roman governors (three of Judaea and one of Greece), Pontius Pilate, Gallio, Festus, and Felix, and the four kings of Judaea, Herod the Great, Herod Antipas, and Herod Agrippa I and II, who, according to the Gospels and Acts, interacted with Jesus and Paul, are well known from the history of Rome and also from the writings of the contemporary Jewish historian Josephus. Some of these interactions enable us to give precise dates to events described in the New Testament. For example, Gallio was governor of Greece for only one year—AD 52; and so Paul's appearance before the law court over which he presided, described in Acts 18: 12–17, must have occurred in that year. Josephus tells the story of John the Baptist, Jesus's predecessor, who baptized him, and mentions Jesus.

It is a basic principle for assessing what other people tell us, a principle which I called in Chapter 1 the **Principle of Testimony**, that it is rational to believe what others tell us (that is, that what others tell us is probably true) unless there is reason to believe otherwise. And likewise we should understand what people say (or write) in its most natural literal sense, again unless there is reason to believe that it is meant to be understood in some less natural sense. Many of the early Christians were killed for refusing to deny Christian doctrines based on the life and teaching of Jesus, which indicates that they had firm beliefs in those doctrines. There are some differences of detail between the different accounts of the life of Jesus; but this is only to be expected when the story of Jesus was transmitted, perhaps mainly by word of mouth, from the main participants to others, and only written up by the others after some twenty to fifty years. In an era when it could take many months to travel from one part of the Mediterranean world to another, and differences in different accounts could not be sorted out by a few emails, such differences are only to be expected.

The extent of **agreement between the various writers** about the main events in the life of Jesus and about his teaching is, however, impressive; and this agreement remains even when, as with the baptism of Jesus by John the Baptist, a main event causes theological problems. The very high view of the status of Jesus as sinless, held by the early Church, implied that he needed no baptism (which was regarded as administered for 'remission of sins'). And yet the synoptic Gospels all recorded the baptism of Jesus, even though Matthew's account makes an attempt to explain why it happened despite Jesus's sinless status. The Gospel accounts of what Jesus taught also overlap substantially with the only account of that teaching outside the New Testament which has a well justified claim to be a significant independent historical source, the 'Gospel of Thomas'. This is a collection of 114 sayings attributed to Jesus put together perhaps in the early second century, about half of which are very similar to sayings recorded in the synoptic Gospels. All of this together indicates that we should take the synoptic Gospels as basically reliable historical sources, to be believed on any matter in the absence of positive reason for believing their account of some particular matter to be false.

It is, however, important to recognize that ancient historians do not have such precise **standards of accuracy** as do modern historians. If they learn that someone delivered a speech with a certain general message, they concoct an apparently verbatim account of such a speech. And they don't necessarily record events in the order in which they occurred. Papias, a bishop at the beginning of the second century, wrote that he was told by 'an elder' that Mark, the author of the Gospel, was Peter's assistant and wrote down accurately all that he remembered of Peter's preaching about Jesus, 'without, however, recording in order the things said or done' by Jesus.

John's Gospel, like the other Gospels, is clearly in broadest outline also seeking to tell us what happened, since the author records most of the same main incidents as the other Gospels; and on two occasions he affirms solemnly that he or his immediate source were witnesses of the events recorded (see, for example, John 19: 35). There are, however, I think, some stories in this Gospel which the author does not intend to be read as history. It does rather look as if, sometimes at least, John tells a story simply as a way of setting forward some deep theological truth. I shall call such a story a 'metaphysical fable.' One obvious example is the story of Jesus's miracle at the pool of Bethesda (John 5: 2–18). Jesus is supposed to have performed a miracle at a pool in Jerusalem where, it is implied, the water was regularly disturbed and the first invalid to get into the water after it was disturbed was healed. The Gospel story tells of Jesus healing someone who was not able to get into the pool in time to be healed in the regular way. Yet if such regular predictable healings occurred, they would be events of a most extraordinary kind of which we know nothing from any other source. The evidence is therefore massively against this healing having happened. Perhaps John was misinformed by some source. But then the Gospel tells us, that the sick man had been sick for thirty-eight years. The people of Israel wandered in the wilderness for thirty-eight years until Joshua ('Joshua' is the Hebrew name for Jesus) led them through the river Jordan to the promised land. No one can read John's Gospel without realizing that symbolism is of immense importance to the author. So plausibly this story is just John's way of telling us that Jesus helps the sick in soul through the water of baptism into the kingdom of Heaven.

In the other Gospels too there are a few stories which we may reasonably suspect of being metaphysical fables, that is ones where the author purports to record a deed or remark of Jesus which he does not believe that Jesus did or said in a literal sense, but which, in his view, expresses the essence of what Jesus was doing or teaching. Perhaps some parts of the 'Infancy narratives', the stories of Jesus's birth contained in Matthew and Luke, are of this kind. But in general, for the reasons I have given, the Gospels are seeking to tell us literally true history and we should believe them, in the absence of positive evidence for supposing either that the author did not intend what he wrote to be understood literally, or that there is reason to suppose that, although the author intended what he wrote to be taken literally, the event recounted probably did not happen and so the author was misled. I emphasize that at this stage in the argument I am treating the Bible, and in particular the New Testament, simply as an ordinary historical document written by ordinary human authors whose truth or falsity is to be assessed by normal historical methods. Later in the book we shall consider whether and how far it should be treated as having a much higher status, as 'inspired Scripture'.

The Miracles of Jesus and the Virgin Birth

The major reason which many people have for supposing that some Gospel incidents did not occur is that, if they had occurred, they would have been violations of laws of nature. Many stories in the Gospels which are called '**miracle stories**' may not involve violations of laws of nature, and so may not be miracles in my sense. We don't know enough about the previous condition of many of those purportedly cured by Jesus to know whether the cure would have involved a violation of laws of nature. Maybe the son of the widow of Nain was not really dead when Jesus told him to get up (Luke 7: 11–17). And people do sometimes recover from fever suddenly, and so the recovery of Peter's mother-in-law (Mark 1: 30–1) need not have involved a violation of natural laws. But there do seem to be some miracle stories in the Gospels which, if correctly reported, involve violations of laws of nature; for example, the healing of the withered hand (Mark 3: 1–6) or the instantaneous recovery from leprosy (Mark 1: 40–5). We know enough about the laws of physiology to know that they would have to be set aside for withered hands to grow again suddenly, or leprosy to disappear instantaneously. And there are many other cures recorded in the Gospels which, if they occurred as described, are also quite probably violations. If the laws of nature are the ultimate determinants of what happens, then, as I wrote in the previous chapter, it is immensely unlikely that such events occurred. But if there is a God, he makes the laws of nature operate and can set them aside if and when he chooses and perform a miracle or allow someone else to do so.

Why would God choose to allow Jesus to work various miracles? Perhaps simply out of compassion for particular suffering people. But perhaps also in order to put his signature on the work of Jesus, in the way indicated in Chapter 6. However, even if we have good reason for believing that there is a God who can set aside the laws of nature, we should not believe that he has done so on a particular occasion without substantial historical evidence that an event occurred which is such that, if it had occurred, would have been a violation of laws of nature. For clearly, if miracles occur, they occur only very rarely. In the case of all the New Testament miracles except one, we do not have lists of witnesses and physical evidence about what happened. The one exception for which we do have quite a bit of such evidence is the Resurrection of Jesus; I shall argue in Chapter 8 that the Resurrection really happened. If I am right that the life of Jesus concludes with this all-important miracle, that makes it much more probable that the other lesser miracles associated with his life also occurred. And the Gospel writers claim that Jesus performed very many cures other than those recorded in the Gospels. If God associated one miracle with the life of Jesus, he might well associate others, both in order to confirm his signature on that life, and also—since most of the purported miracles were purported miracles of healing—to show us that, while there are good reasons for God to allow human suffering, it was his plan that such suffering should come to an end as a result of the work of Jesus.

There is, however, one other purported miracle not brought about by Jesus but associated with his life and recorded in the Gospels (Matthew 1: 18 and Luke 1: 34–5), which the Church thought so important that it is included as a central Christian doctrine in the Creed: the **Virgin Birth**. The doctrine holds that Jesus was conceived in the womb of his mother, 'the Virgin Mary', not as the result of sexual intercourse; Jesus had no human father. It claims that the Holy Spirit brought about this conception, and, of course, God would have needed to intervene to bring this about, since the laws of physiology require male sperm to fertilize a female egg. I claimed in Chapter 3 that there was some prior probability that God might symbolize God becoming human by there being only one human contribution (the female one) to the fertilized embryo which became the human Jesus; and this would then be a further divine signature on the life of Jesus—a signature at the beginning as well as at the end of that life.

But, as with the other purported miracles apart from the Resurrection, **there is a shortage of witnesses and physical evidence**. Matthew and Luke give accounts of Jesus's birth otherwise very different from each other and for which they clearly had very different sources. (And the fact of the same claim—of the Virgin Birth—being made in two very different accounts indicates that Matthew and Luke were not recounting a metaphysical fable.) However, these sources could themselves have had at most one fully reliable source of the story of the Virgin Birth, Mary herself. Although she would have been dead by the time the Gospels were written, she could have told her story to Matthew and Luke's sources, or to others who told these sources. There is no other reference in the New Testament to the Virgin Birth (nor any passage denying it). But I think that there are **two reasons why**, if it is true, **the story might have surfaced only later** than the first few years after the death of Jesus. The first such reason is that Christians saw it as their immediate task after (what they believed to be) Jesus's Resurrection to convince the Jews that Jesus was God's special messenger who had risen from the dead. They were therefore keen to publicize only events for which good witness evidence could be produced, and, as we will see in Chapter 8, the testimony of one woman did not in the view of contemporary Jews constitute good witness evidence. And that would be so especially if the story would look like a way of covering up a more obvious explanation of Mary becoming pregnant before Mary and Joseph lived together, that Jesus had a human father other than Joseph. (And in the second century Jewish opponents of Christianity did claim that Jesus was illegitimate. They may have claimed this then as a reaction to the story of the Virgin Birth.) And the second reason why the story might have surfaced only later is that, until an enormously high view of the status of Jesus developed in the Church, Mary would surely have seen that she would not be believed, and so was anxious to escape ridicule or the charge of having had sexual intercourse before marriage. Luke claims that at first Mary 'pondered' what had happened 'in her heart' (Luke 2: 19 and 51).

There is a lot more to be said about the historical evidence for and against the Virgin Birth. But if you do not on other grounds think it moderately probable that there is a God (which I assume in this book) likely to intervene in history by becoming incarnate and to show that he has done so (for which I have argued in Part I), you must surely conclude that the historical evidence is inadequate. But if you agree that it is moderately probable that there is a God who would intervene in history by becoming incarnate, and also that there is significant evidence of God's signature on the life of Jesus at its end in his Resurrection, then that increases significantly the probability that God provided a (less evident) signature on the life of Jesus also at its beginning. And, I shall argue in Chapter 11, this probability of the Virgin Birth will be further increased by the very fact of it being taught as a central item of Church doctrine for 1,700 years, the Church's authority also being guaranteed—as I shall argue in later chapters—by the Resurrection.

So, given that, as I have argued, the New Testament is a basically reliable source of information about the life of Jesus, I am going to show that our historical evidence is such as we would expect if that life were characterized by the non-miraculous features which I listed at the beginning of this chapter. These features are the features which it was (at least) probable that a prophet's life would show if he were God Incarnate: that he led a perfect human life in which there was much suffering; that he claimed to be God Incarnate; claimed to be making atonement for our sins; gave plausible purportedly revealed teaching about the nature of God, how we should live our lives, and his plans for our future; and founded a Church to continue his work. (There was also the further feature that the Church which he founded should give plausible interpretations of his teaching, and I will come to consider that later in the book.)

Jesus Led a Perfect Life Involving Suffering

The first requirement for Jesus to be God Incarnate is that the life of Jesus was a perfect human life which involved much suffering. The evidence for the goodness of another person's life can, of course, come only from their public behaviour. But I suggest that such evidence as there is of Jesus's public behaviour is what we would expect if he led a perfect human life. One aspect of this, that Jesus **ate with society's outcasts** as well as eating with the Pharisees, seems virtually undisputed. On this it is appropriate to quote the distinguished Jewish scholar Geza Vermes:

In one respect more than any other [Jesus] differed from both his contemporaries and even his prophetic predecessors. The prophets spoke on behalf of the honest poor, and defended the widows and the fatherless, those oppressed and exploited by the wicked, rich and powerful. Jesus went further. In addition to proclaiming these blessed, he actually took his stand among the pariahs of his world, those despised by the respectable. Sinners were his table-companions and the ostracized tax-collectors and prostitutes his friends.   (Geza Vermes, *Jesus the Jew*, SCM Press, 1994, 196)

Tax collectors were notorious for trying to extract from citizens more than the taxes which they were authorized by the Roman authorities to collect. But when Jesus went to stay with the tax collector Zacchaeus, people complained, 'He has gone to be the guest of one who is a sinner' (Luke 19: 7), and that before Zacchaeus had announced his intention of changing his lifestyle. Jesus showed the love of God towards all.

Like John the Baptist, he did not reserve his instruction for committed disciples, but taught publicly anyone willing to listen. To **teach people** about God, his love towards them, and how they should live is obviously a good thing if what is taught is true, and I will come to that soon. **Prayer** and religious experience played an important part in the life of Jesus, and, given that there is a God, it is a mark of perfection that this should play an important part in a life. The fact that Jesus **sought baptism from John the Baptist** would only suggest that he considered himself a sinner, if baptism was administered, as it was in the Christian Church within a few years of its foundation, solely for the remission of the sin of the person seeking baptism. But it is not at all evident that John's baptism had that character (and the Jewish historian Josephus explicitly denied that it had that character); someone might seek baptism simply in order to identify himself with sinful Israelites and their need for remission of sins. (Paul, in 1 Corinthians 15: 29, mentions the practice, which soon died out, of people being baptized on behalf of other people who were already dead.)

During the three years of his ministry, the life of Jesus was the life of a wandering teacher, and there seems no reason to doubt the genuineness of his saying abut himself that 'the Son of Man has nowhere to lay his head'. His life ended with his **Crucifixion**, instigated by the Jewish leaders and carried out by the Romans. All the Gospel accounts of the 'Passion' (Jesus's betrayal, arrest, trial, and Crucifixion) are keen to emphasize that he voluntarily allowed himself to be arrested under circumstances where death was a likely outcome. He thus showed his total dedication to changing people by rational persuasion rather than by force of arms.

I shall comment in the next section on the fact that the charge against Jesus at his trial before the Jewish leaders was that of blasphemy; and I shall argue that we must understand 'blasphemy' as claiming rights that belonged to God alone. So if, as I am arguing, Jesus was indeed God Incarnate, he did nothing wrong in claiming these rights. The Gospels all claim that the charge on which the Jewish authorities asked the Roman governor, Pontius Pilate, to condemn Jesus to death was that he made himself 'the King of the Jews'. And there is every reason to suppose that the Gospels did not invent this, since this phrase 'King of the Jews' was never used of Jesus by Jews or anyone else in the Gospel accounts of his life before that moment (and it was not the title used of the Herods mentioned above). But the '**Messiah**' means the future King of Israel whose coming the Jews awaited. If, as the Gospel accounts assert, Jesus did claim in his trial before the Jewish leaders to be the Messiah, the best way in which those leaders could explain this to Pilate, a Roman ignorant of Jewish religion, was that what Jesus was claiming was that he was 'King of the Jews'. This was, however, a claim which Pilate could all too easily misunderstand. He would easily suppose that someone who claimed to be a king was planning to overthrow the Roman authorities by force—and there is not the slightest reason to suppose that Jesus was planning to do that.

So the claims which Jesus made were (if he was God Incarnate) claims which he had the right to make, and so the sentence of death imposed on him by the Roman governor at the instigation of the Jewish authorities was the condemnation of an innocent man. To die by the judicial sentence of crucifixion when innocent of the charges on which he was condemned did indeed involve his life ending in a way in which there was much suffering. See especially the Gospel accounts of his 'agony' in the Garden of Gethsemane before his arrest and trial. He shared the pain and injustice of human life in a big way. The Gospels make it clear that he deliberately chose to allow himself to suffer this pain and injustice.

Jesus Claimed to Be Divine

When the Gospel writers report Jesus himself referring to himself as 'Son of God', this did not in New Testament times mean what it came to mean in later Christian theology (as I described this in Chapter 3) or carry any implication that Jesus was divine; it may simply mean 'Messiah' or even just 'a righteous person'. Nevertheless, despite the fact that the majority of New Testament scholars hold the opposite opinion, I suggest that in other ways the historical evidence of the actions as well as the words of Jesus are such as we would expect if Jesus did teach that he was divine.

These scholars are, I believe, correct in holding that **Jesus did not say explicitly** and openly **during his earthly life** (before whatever happened after his Crucifixion) 'I am God'. But there is a reason why Jesus could not make a claim to be divine in such a direct way during his earthly life. If God was to become incarnate for the purposes I have discussed, he needed to take a human nature (a human way of thinking and acting) and a human body in addition to his divine nature, in the way defined by the Council of Chalcedon. This is a difficult concept to grasp. If Jesus had announced during his earthly ministry 'I am God', this would have been understood as a claim to be a pagan god, a powerful and lustful being who had temporarily occupied a human body, and not the all-good source of all being. The Jewish scholar Geza Vermes writes that 'it is no exaggeration to contend that the identification of a contemporary historical figure with God would have been inconceivable to a first-century AD Palestinian Jew' (*Jesus the Jew*, 185).

Vermes's point means that the failure of Jesus to say 'I am God' during his lifetime is not evidence that he did not believe himself to be God. This is a message which Jesus could begin to proclaim openly only after his Crucifixion had made very plain the reality of his humanity and so the kind of God he would have to have been; and after the Resurrection had provided evidence of his unique status.

And there is evidence that, given that Jesus rose from the dead (as I shall argue in Chapter 8), **he proclaimed his divinity more openly after his Resurrection**. Matthew's Gospel ends with Jesus commanding 'the Eleven' (that is, the original twelve disciples minus Judas, who had betrayed Jesus) to baptize 'in the name of the Father, and of the Son, and of the Holy Spirit' (Matthew 28: 19). This saying puts 'the Son' (Jesus) on a level with God the Father. Critics have suggested that this verse was not in the original text of the Gospel; but all manuscripts of the Gospel contain this verse, and so it must have been in the text from an early stage. Then John's Gospel records the explicit confession by the formerly doubting, now convinced, Thomas of Jesus as 'My Lord and my God' (John 20: 28), a confession which Jesus did not reject.

On two post-Resurrection occasions Matthew's Gospel records that **disciples 'worshipped'** Jesus; and many ancient manuscripts of Luke's Gospel record a similar 'worship' by the eleven (Luke 24: 52). The New Testament writers considered that it would be wrong to worship anyone who was not God. Thus, both Matthew and Luke report Jesus as quoting the Old Testament command 'Worship the Lord your God and serve only him', in response to the Devil's invitation to worship him (the Devil). In Acts 10: 26 Peter stops Cornelius worshipping him with the words 'Stand up: I am only a mortal'. And twice in the New Testament book of Revelation the angel commands John (the purported author of the book which records his vision) not to worship him with the words 'You must not do that! I am a fellow servant with you . . . Worship God'. Jesus, on the other hand, is never reported as rejecting worship; and Matthew's Gospel does record also some pre-Resurrection occurrences of worship of Jesus. This evidence is such as we would expect if Jesus were God Incarnate, even if liberal critics claim that it can be accounted for by the Gospel writers reading such claims back into history in the light of the Church's later beliefs.

As Jesus could only claim his divinity explicitly after his Resurrection, and as even then it might not be easily comprehensible
by his followers, he would need also to make the claim during his
earthly life by means of his public actions and by means of public
teaching in which this claim was contained implicitly, reflection
on which could lead his followers after his life was finished to see
what he was claiming. And I think that **Jesus did claim divinity by
his actions and (implicitly) by his words during his earthly life**.

This can be seen by the fact that the charge against Jesus at
his trial before the Jewish leaders was, according to Mark and
Matthew, that of **blasphemy**. Clearly Jesus did not curse God, and
so his 'blasphemy' must mean that he claimed to do things which
God alone could do. This is the way John's Gospel understood that
accusation. John records that the Jews attempted to stone Jesus,
saying, 'It is not for a good work that we are going to stone you,
but for blasphemy, because you, though only a human being, are
making yourself God' (John 10: 33).

According to the synoptic Gospels, two issues were raised at the
trial of Jesus before Caiaphas, both relevant to the accusation of
blasphemy. Jesus was asked whether he was the Messiah. Claiming
to be the Messiah would not in itself be claiming to do what God
alone had the right to do. But Jesus's reply, quoting Daniel 7: 13, 'You
will see the Son of Man [a term which Jesus used elsewhere to refer
to himself] seated at the right hand of power', and 'coming with the
clouds of Heaven', was **claiming a very high kind of Messiahship**;
and it was to that comment that, according to Mark, Caiaphas
responded with 'You have heard his blasphemy.' Now again it is
not obvious that even this remark of Jesus is claiming divinity;
and critics have claimed that even Jesus's explicit confession of
Messiahship at this time was Mark's invention.

But the other issue raised at the trial is more interesting, because
Mark claims that the witness testimony was false and so it is hardly
his invention. Mark and Matthew record that witnesses testified
that Jesus said that he would or could **destroy the Temple and
build in three days 'another Temple not made with hands'**.
John too quotes Jesus as saying, 'Destroy this temple, and in three
days I will raise it up' (John 2: 1). The liberal biblical scholar
E. P. Sanders writes, 'It is hard to imagine a purely fictional origin
for the accusation that [Jesus] threatened to destroy the Temple'
(E. P. Sanders, *Jesus and Judaism*, SCM Press, 1985, 72). Mark

described this accusation as 'false'. But Mark's Gospel may well have been written after AD 70 and then he would have known that the Temple was destroyed by the Romans in that year; and in any case he records elsewhere (Mark 13: 2) a further prediction by Jesus of its destruction, which implies that he (Mark) believed that it would be destroyed. So the falsity of the accusation (in Mark's view) must lie in one of two things: Jesus did not threaten to destroy the Temple himself, but merely predicted that it would be destroyed; and/or he did not promise to build another in three days. But Mark believed that he did build in three days something else which had been destroyed, that is, himself, which, when the Temple was destroyed, Christians regarded as a replacement for it. (The Letter to the Hebrews (9: 11) describes Jesus as coming 'as a high priest' through the 'greater and more perfect tent [i.e. Temple], not made with hands'.) So the falsity of the witnesses' accusation is more likely to consist in the fact that Jesus did not threaten to destroy the Temple but merely predicted that it would be destroyed by someone else and not himself. To replace the divinely instituted worship of the Temple with another kind of worship was clearly God's privilege; and Jesus is not reported as saying that God had commissioned him to do this—he is reported as saying that he would do it himself. And that is a claim to divinity.

Another way in which Jesus made his claim to divinity was by forgiving sins. The Gospels record two occasions on which Jesus **forgave sins**. On one of these occasions the scribes who saw this are reported to have said 'Why does this fellow speak in this way? It is blasphemy! Who can forgive sins but God alone?' (Mark 2: 7).

As well as claiming divinity, Jesus showed himself to be **fully human**, acting in ignorance and weakness, and being subject to temptation. Luke's Gospel claims that the boy Jesus 'increased in wisdom' (Luke 2: 52), that is, grew in knowledge, which seems to imply that he was not always fully omniscient. Likewise, in Mark's Gospel Jesus is reported as claiming that he, 'the Son', does not know something which the Father does know: 'the day or hour' at which 'Heaven and Earth will pass away'. And Jesus's cry of dereliction from the Cross, 'My God, my God, why have you forsaken me?' (Mark 15: 34), might seem to suggest that Jesus at that moment ceased to believe that God was sustaining him. There is a passage in Mark that casts similar doubt on Jesus's omnipotence. It reports that in a visit to the region of Palestine where he grew up, Jesus 'could do no deed of power there' (Mark 6: 5). That Jesus was subject to temptations is made explicit by the accounts in the synoptic Gospels of the temptations at the beginning of his ministry. And there are passages in the Letter to the Hebrews which imply that the temptations to which he was subject were ones to which he could have yielded but did not yield. He is said to have been 'in every respect . . . tested as we are, yet without sin' (Hebrews 4: 15), to have 'learned obedience through what he suffered', and to have been 'made perfect' (i.e. over time) (Hebrews 5: 8–9). All of this indicates that, if Jesus was God Incarnate, God was incarnate in Jesus in the way described in Chapter 3: by taking a human nature separate from his divine nature. His human actions were done in ignorance and weakness and subject to temptation.

Jesus Claimed to Make Atonement for Human Sins

On this issue my views are in much greater agreement with New Testament scholars. I have just argued that Jesus claimed that he would provide a replacement for the Temple; the function of the Temple was to offer sacrifices to God, a major purpose of which was to achieve atonement for sin. And then there is the **Last Supper** (the first eucharist), a solemn meal at Passover time, in which Jesus gave to his disciples bread and wine with the words 'This is my body' and 'This is my blood'. Body and blood are the elements of sacrifice. Jesus is telling his disciples that his life is a sacrifice. (The eucharist or Communion service is the regular, normally at least weekly, ceremony of the Christian Church at which its members receive bread and wine over which have been pronounced the words of Jesus at the Last Supper.)

All the New Testament accounts of the Last Supper regard it as a 'new' covenant, and the writers knew that the Old Testament prophet Jeremiah had prophesied a 'new covenant' which he connected with 'the forgiveness of sins' (Jeremiah 31: 31–4). At the beginning of the last week of his life, Jesus had challenged the Jewish authorities in a big way. But he took pains to keep out of trouble (not sleeping in Jerusalem, and making arrangements for the Last Supper to be kept secret from most of the Twelve) until after the Last Supper, when he was betrayed. He then allowed himself to be arrested. Jesus died on the Cross either on the day of the Passover or on the day after it, and in the latter case it was the eucharist which was instituted on Passover Day. The Passover was the annual commemoration of the Exodus of the Jews from Egypt. As the Exodus involved an escape from slavery, so—various books of the New Testament claim—did the death of Jesus and what happened after it, yet not slavery to a literal foreign power, but to sinfulness, guilt, and death. If Jesus allowed himself to be crucified at Passover time subsequently to instituting the eucharist, he inevitably proclaimed in the contemporary culture an understanding of it of this kind. I conclude that the claim of many New Testament books, that Jesus 'died for our sins', originated in the teaching of Jesus.

Jesus Provided Plausible 'Revealed' Teaching on God and Morality

Jesus assumed in his teaching that God was the all-powerful, all-knowing creator of the world. He taught people that God loves them, that they should forgive each other and show unlimited love to each other, should worship God, and ask him for good things. Jesus told people to **rely on God** to provide good things, bodily and spiritual. It is difficult to interpret the parables told by Jesus of the prodigal son, the lost sheep, and the lost coin, except as showing (among other things) the **great love of God for humans**; as does Jesus's explicit teaching about how much God loves us more than the lilies and the birds, on whom he also bestows love (Matthew 6: 26). That **we should forgive each other** 'not seven times, but, I tell you, seventy-seven times' is the way Matthew reports Jesus's teaching on forgiveness. That God is the master who forgives us much and expects us to forgive the lesser wrongs which others have done to us is the obvious application of the parable of two servants, drawn out explicitly by Matthew (18: 23–35). This is borne out by the obviously remembered Lord's prayer, where the disciples were told to pray, 'Forgive us our debts, as we have also forgiven our debtors': we should forgive others before we can ask God's forgiveness for ourselves. That we should show great love to others is, more than anything else, the theme of the Sermon on the Mount and of the parable of the sheep and goats. **We are to love** our enemies, go the extra mile, lend without expecting a return, feed the hungry, clothe the naked, visit the sick and imprisoned, etc.

Jesus also certainly endorsed the more detailed Old Testament teaching contained in the **Ten Commandments** about certain minimum ways in which we should show that love: that we should worship God alone; reverence our parents; and not steal, murder, commit adultery, or lie in a court of law. The observance of **prayer, fasting, and almsgiving**, with a proper attitude of humility before God and avoiding using these as a means of acquiring a good reputation on earth, are also evident themes of Jesus's teaching. So too is honesty, and thus the avoidance of hypocrisy. It is, he taught, more important to show love to those in need than to conform to exact details of ritual.

Although Jesus seems to have commended observing the Jewish Law about matters of ritual and sacrifice (contained in such Old Testament books as the book of Leviticus), it is unclear just how important he though that. Jesus did, however, teach that **following himself** was more important than observing the Law; if he was indeed divine, this would follow from the duty to serve God. The apostolic Church regarded itself as inspired by the Holy Spirit to deem that Christians need no longer conform to these Old Testament requirements of sacrifice and ritual (see Acts 15: 28–9), and it must have thought that this declaration was in the spirit of Jesus's teaching. (I shall henceforward understand 'the Apostolic Church' not as the Church deriving from the Apostles, which is the way it is understood in the Creed (see pp. 75–6), but simply as the Church of the Apostles, that is the Church of the first twenty or so years after the death of Jesus, centred on the original Church leaders, the twelve Apostles.) As I claimed in Chapter 5, almost everyone would agree that the way of living towards God and our fellows which Jesus commended is a good way to live. So all this is the sort of teaching one would expect God Incarnate to give. Jesus presented his teaching as coming from God.

As with the later Church teaching, it is unclear just how much of Jesus's teaching concerns our moral obligations and how much is simply advice about how to become morally perfect, but it does seem that some of his more demanding teaching concerns our moral obligations. I pointed out in Chapter 1 that God has the right to command us to do certain actions which would not be otherwise obligatory, but which, if God commands us to do them, would become obligatory. I argued in Chapter 5 that we might expect God to issue such commands for two reasons, and thereby help us to become naturally good people. An all-important example of this more demanding teaching is Jesus's interpretation of the command of God reported in the Old Testament, 'You shall love your neighbour as yourself'. In answer to the question 'And who is my neighbour?' Jesus told the parable of the Good Samaritan (Luke 10: 29–37), with its clear message that one's neighbour is anyone, fellow citizen or foreigner, with whom one is in contact. So interpreted the command is **very demanding**, and a command imposes an obligation. Those who obey the command will be trying to conform to that higher standard of morality which God would want to become natural to us, so that we should become naturally loving people.

Jesus is recorded as having given only one very detailed new piece of instruction on our moral obligations. This concerns **divorce**. Mark 10: 10–12 (and Luke 16: 18) seems to constitute an absolute ban on divorce; Matthew 5: 32 states that the ban on divorce applies except in the case of 'unchastity' (*porneia*). It is disputed whether Jesus actually made this exception (or whether it is an addition to his teaching reflecting the practice of Matthew's local church). It is also disputed what exactly *porneia* means in this context; many later Christians have understood it to mean 'adultery', and so have understood Jesus as allowing someone to divorce a spouse who has been unfaithful. But, however *porneia* is understood, clearly Jesus forbade divorce merely on the grounds that husband and wife both want it; and I gave an argument in Chapter 5 claiming that it is plausible that God might wish to forbid that.

Jesus taught that there will be a '**Parousia**', that is, the world will come to an end (although he refused to name an exact date at which this would occur); all humans would be raised from the dead, and there would be a 'Last Judgement', at which God would divide the good from the bad. God would take the good to himself (in **Heaven**) and banish the wicked from him to **Hell**. The standard of behaviour for getting to Heaven was a high one. Jesus seems to have taught that the separation of the good and the bad would be permanent. He describes the fate of the wicked as 'destruction', or 'loss' of the 'bridegroom' (Jesus himself) or of good things. Sometimes in his parables of the Last Judgement, Jesus spoke of the bad as being cast into a 'fire', but how literally that was to be understood is unclear. This fire is sometimes described as 'eternal' and sometimes as 'unquenchable'. If talk about a fire is to be taken literally or even as an analogy for the destiny of the wicked, the consequence of

putting the wicked in such a fire would be their speedy elimination
(they would be burnt up). Only in one place in the Gospels is
the punishment itself declared to be 'eternal': Matthew 25: 46. Of
course, the point of Jesus preaching all this was to move all people
to repentance, so that there would be no bad left to be punished. I
argued in Chapter 6 that a good God might well allow people the
opportunity permanently to reject him and all that he stands for,
and that inevitably such people would be frustrated and so unhappy
(and if we take talk about being cast into a fire analogically, that
is the state which Jesus is warning people to avoid); and maybe, if
that's what they wish, God would then allow their elimination, as
some of Jesus's words imply would be their ultimate fate.

The situation of those who do not have long enough lives, or
enough understanding of good and bad, to make significant choices
between them is covered by Jesus's parable of two slaves: 'That
slave who knew what his master wanted, but did not prepare himself
or do what was wanted, will receive a severe beating. But one who
did not know and did what deserved a beating will receive a light
beating' (Luke 12: 47–8). There will be no Hell for those who do
not fully realize what they were doing.

Finally, in his teaching about God we should note that Jesus is
reported to have said some things relevant to the doctrine of **the
Trinity**, which—I claimed in Chapter 2—there is good a priori
reason to suppose to be true. It is not a good objection to the claim
that Jesus believed this doctrine that he did not teach it explicitly;
for, if a claim by Jesus to be God, made before his Crucifixion,
would almost certainly have been misunderstood, any explicit
assertion of the doctrine of the Trinity would without any doubt
have been understood as a proclamation of the polytheism believed
by ordinary Greeks and Romans. But there are two kinds of thing
which Jesus is reported as having said which provided the later
Church with material to develop that doctrine. First, while acting
so as to imply his divinity, Jesus nevertheless clearly **distinguished
himself sharply from God the Father**. Luke cites Jesus as saying,
'All things have been handed over to me by my Father; and no
one knows who the Son is except the Father, or who the Father
is except the Son and anyone to whom the Son chooses to reveal
him'; and he addresses God the Father as another person, 'Father'.

Secondly, there is much material in the New Testament about
the work of the **Holy Spirit**, some of which certainly seems to

derive from the teaching of Jesus. Mark and Matthew report Jesus at his baptism as having seen the Spirit descending on him in the form of a dove; Luke simply reports that the Spirit did descend. Thereafter, according to all three synoptic Gospels, the Spirit drove Jesus into the wilderness to be tempted. The disciples would not have known of the latter unless Jesus had told them, and it looks as if the Spirit was recognized at his baptism only by Jesus himself; and so he too is the source of their belief about this feature of his baptism. Acts 1 records that Jesus after his Resurrection promised to his Apostles the guidance of the Holy Spirit, in consequence of which they would be his witnesses 'in Jerusalem, in all Judaea and Samaria, and to the ends of the earth'; and Acts 2 tells of the work of the Holy Spirit in inspiring the multilingual speaking of the disciples at Pentecost. None of this, however, implies that the Spirit was personal. John's Gospel (chapters 14–17), however, contains a very lengthy passage of teaching attributed to Jesus, about the work which the 'Holy Spirit' will do in the Church after Jesus is no longer among the disciples in bodily form. In this passage Jesus distinguishes 'the Spirit', whom he also calls 'the Advocate', from 'the Father' and 'the Son'. And this passage does imply that the Spirit is personal, for although the Greek word for 'spirit' is neuter in gender (and so Greeks thought of 'spirit' as a thing and not a person), Jesus is reported as sometimes referring to the Spirit by the masculine pronoun 'he'.

And finally, the command of Jesus at the end of St Matthew's Gospel, quoted earlier, puts 'the Spirit' on a level with the Son and the Father. Although some of this Gospel material may not derive directly from the teaching of Jesus but rather from the subsequent reflection of the early Church, the quantity and distribution (in all four Gospels) of the material does make it fairly probable that Jesus had given some teaching about the Spirit. Jesus presented much of this teaching as a new message from God. I argued in Part I that all this teaching is in my sense 'plausible', that is, such that it is not very improbable that it is true teaching.

Jesus Founded a Church

Jesus appointed **twelve** 'Apostles'. That there were twelve chief followers of Jesus is referred to in many New Testament writings, though the lists of the Twelve in the Gospels differ slightly from each other. (That then were twelve chief followers was so firmly fixed in the minds of the New Testament writers, that-as we shall see in the next chapter-when Judas had betrayed Jesus and only eleven remained. The post-Resurrection narratives still often refer to those eleven as 'the Twelve'.) The old Israel deriving from Abraham had (in the common belief of first-century Jews) twelve tribes deriving from twelve tribe-founding individuals. A Jewish prophet who founded a community based on twelve leaders had to be understood to be claiming to found a new, reformed Israel. Further, as already noted, Jesus instituted at the 'Last Supper' a ceremony in which he and the original Twelve were the first participants, the eucharist; and all subsequent Christian communities were characterized by regular celebration of the eucharist. These two acts constitute solemn actions of founding a new, reformed Israel deriving from the Twelve and characterized by a special ceremony. It may be that Jesus expected that the new Israel would absorb the old Israel, or maybe he expected it to continue separately from it—as in fact happened.

The Gospels contain various sayings implying that Jesus or **the Holy Spirit would continue to guide the Church** after his departure. Matthew records twice Jesus's words 'Whatever you bind on earth will be bound in Heaven and whatever you loose on earth will be loosed in Heaven', once (with singular 'you') addressed to Peter and once (with plural 'you') apparently addressed to the whole body of disciples. These words seem to presuppose that the Church would continue the teaching of Jesus (for otherwise people would be bound in Heaven who were more loyal to the teaching of Jesus than was the Church). The final sentence of Matthew's Gospel contains his promise 'I am with you always to the end of the age'. And, as mentioned, there is teaching ascribed to Jesus in John 14–16 promising such continued guidance.

Conclusion

It is true that even if Jesus had not claimed that God would continue to guide the Church after his earthly life was over, Christian writings might well claim that he had. Nevertheless, it is the case that the evidence in this matter, as in all the other matters discussed in this chapter, is such as is to be expected if Jesus was God Incarnate; and the evidence on most of the other matters is not at all to be expected if Jesus was not God Incarnate. In respect of most of the matters discussed in this chapter, while, I have argued, we have reason (by reflecting on what the perfect goodness of God would involve) to expect God to intervene in history through a prophet who behaved in the way that Jesus did, his Jewish contemporaries certainly did not expect God's special messenger (the Messiah) to behave thus. I have already commented that they certainly did not expect him to claim the right to do things which God alone could do. Also, while many of them expected a priest–Messiah, they certainly didn't expect him to offer the sacrifice of himself. (Passages in the Old Testament which we might interpret as predicting such a sacrifice were not understood by contemporary Jews in this sense.) Indeed there is only one passage in the whole literature of early Judaism (of which there are many books, including the recently discovered Dead Sea Scrolls) in which it is stated that the Messiah (called by that name) will die. This is 2 Esdras 7: 29, which is just a matter-of-fact statement that this will happen; there is no suggestion that the Messiah's death would have any deep significance. That his Jewish contemporaries would not have expected a Messiah to behave in the way that Jesus did is reason to suppose that the Gospels are not reading back into history what the Jews would have expected to find.

I conclude that the evidence which I have cited about the life and teaching of Jesus is such as it is quite probable we would find if Jesus lived a perfect life with much suffering, claimed to be God Incarnate and to be making atonement for human sins, gave plausible teaching (as a revelation) on morality and God, and founded a Church. It is very improbable that we would have most of the evidence we do if Jesus did not live and teach in this way; it is, for example, very improbable that we would have the New Testament reports of the Last Supper that we do unless Jesus was claiming to provide atonement for our sins. Hence, the evidence strongly supports this account of the life and teaching of Jesus.

8 THE RESURRECTION OF JESUS

I argued in the previous chapter that our evidence about the life and teaching of Jesus is such as it is probable we would find if his life were the sort of life and teaching that God Incarnate would live and teach, and very improbable we would find otherwise. But that is not enough to show that Jesus was God Incarnate. For it is not very improbable that in the course of human history given the large number of different kinds of humans there might have appeared by chance just once a prophet who lived the requisite sort of life and gave the requisite sort of teaching, but who was nevertheless just an ordinary human. As I argued in Chapter 6, to establish that a prophet was God Incarnate we need also God's signature on the prophet's work. Someone's signature on a work is an event which can (with high probability) only be brought about by that person, and occurs in connection with the work in a way which the culture in which it occurs would recognize as an endorsement of that work.

An obvious event which can be brought about by God alone is (if there is a God) any violation of laws of nature; such a violation, if brought about by God, I am calling a miracle. The Gospels claim that Jesus, who was by normal criteria dead, came to life again on the first Easter Day (the Sunday after the Friday on which he died) in such a condition as to appear and disappear at will. Although we do not know everything about the laws of physiology, we know enough to know that this would indeed be a violation of natural laws, and so, if brought about by God, a miracle. I shall argue later in this chapter that it would be an event of a kind which the contemporary culture would recognize as God's signature on the work of Jesus. There is, I now claim, significant detailed historical evidence of the Resurrection of Jesus. If Jesus rose bodily from the dead on the first Easter Day, we would expect two sorts of witness evidence: witnesses who talked with a person whom they took to be Jesus, and witnesses who saw the empty tomb.

The Appearances of the Risen Jesus

Matthew, Luke, John, Acts, and 1 Corinthians provide lists of witnesses who, they claim, talked with Jesus subsequently to his death on the Cross. The earliest text of **Mark**'s Gospel is generally agreed to have ended at 16: 8 with the story of the women finding the empty tomb, and before anyone met the risen Jesus. (16: 9–20 is a later addition summarizing what is recorded in other Gospels, primarily Luke.) But the earlier parts of Mark contain three separate predictions of the Resurrection, and Mark 16: 7 reports a 'young man' in white telling the women who found the empty tomb that Jesus was risen and would meet them in Galilee. So Mark certainly believed that Jesus appeared to his disciples after his Resurrection, and to my mind the most probable explanation of why the earliest text we have of his Gospel ended at 16: 8 is that there is a lost ending. The last part of the manuscript was lost, and so Mark 16: 9–20 was added by some later scribe to summarize some main appearances of Jesus recorded in the other Gospels.

The earliest list of witnesses to whom Jesus appeared is that given by Paul in 1 **Corinthians** (15: 3–8), which—he reminded the Corinthians he had conveyed to them previously—and which he himself had 'received' (apart, that is, presumably, from what he also lists here: Jesus's appearance to himself). This list records that Jesus appeared first to Peter (whom Paul calls 'Cephas'), then to 'the Twelve', then to 'above five hundred brothers and sisters at one time, most of whom are still alive, though some have died', then to James, then to all the Apostles, and finally to Paul himself 'as to one untimely born'. The implication of the latter phrase is that the appearance to Paul was much later than the other appearances.

Two of the Gospels, however, begin with **one appearance earlier than the appearance to Peter**, the first appearance listed by Paul. Matthew reports that Jesus appeared to Mary Magdalene and 'the other Mary' at the empty tomb on the first Easter morning; and John (chapter 20) reports that he appeared to Mary Magdalene then. The third relevant Gospel, Luke, reports that Jesus had a long conversation that same evening with a disciple called Cleopas and another disciple, walking from Jerusalem to Emmaus (some 7 miles); they only recognized him when he came to eat with them at Emmaus, blessed bread, and then disappeared. Luke does not make it clear whether this appearance occurred before or after an appearance to Peter, which Luke claims to have occurred in Jerusalem also on the first Easter evening.

Luke lists a further appearance in Jerusalem to the 'Eleven'(and their companions) also on the first Easter evening but after the two other appearances. This latter appearance began with Jesus eating in front of them (to show that he was not a ghost) and ends with Jesus being 'carried up into the sky' (his literal 'ascension'). Matthew also lists an appearance in Galilee to the Eleven. John 20 lists also the appearance to the disciples in Jerusalem on the first Easter evening, and a second one a week later. John 21, which seems to be a chapter written separately before being added on to the main body of the Gospel, records an appearance to seven disciples, five of them including Peter and John being named, in Galilee. Acts begins with the claim that Jesus 'presented himself alive to [the Apostles] by many convincing proofs, appearing to them over the course of forty days and speaking about the kingdom of God', and continues with a detailed story of Jesus's literal 'ascension' in the presence of his Apostles. Later sermons of Peter and Paul reported in Acts renew the claim that Jesus was seen for many days by many disciples; Peter's sermon claims that Jesus 'ate and drank' with his disciples on these occasions.

As I have illustrated, our sources give somewhat different lists of who saw Jesus where and when; and this is often thought to be a major difficulty casting doubt on the whole story. There is, however, an important reason for most of the **differences about who saw Jesus**, between Paul's list in 1 Corinthians, and the Gospel lists. 1 Corinthians has the form of a credal statement, an official Church-recognized list of 'witnesses', which was in existence well before Paul wrote it down. The list therefore contains only people whom the Jews (at whom Christian preaching was first directed) would take seriously. The Jews would not take women witnesses seriously. The contemporary Jewish writer Josephus states that Moses prohibited recognizing women as witnesses. Hence no mention of Mary Magdalene or 'the other Mary' in the official list. Cleopas was not a senior Church leader, and his companion may well have been his wife, apparently mentioned in John 19: 25 as being present at the Crucifixion. The Gospels, being written later (when Jewish attitudes had hardened) and being more interested in precisely who did see Jesus than in providing an official list of witnesses, put things differently. And Matthew and John certainly wouldn't have recorded that women were the first witnesses of the Resurrection, before the appearance to the leader of the Church, Peter, unless they were convinced that that is what happened.

There seems also to be a **difference between the sources about where the appearances took place.** Matthew claims that Jesus appeared to the Eleven in Galilee; and Mark recorded a prediction that he would do. But this seems to be in conflict with the account in Luke 24. Luke seems to date the three appearances which he records as all taking place on the first Easter Day in Jerusalem; and his account of these is followed, as I noted, by an account of Jesus's literal 'ascension'. But I do not think that we should regard Luke as claiming that the ascension occurred immediately after Jesus's first appearance to 'the Eleven'. This is because it would then be in direct conflict with Acts, written by the same author. Acts 1:3 and 13:31 speak of Jesus appearing for 'forty' or 'many' days after his Resurrection. This suggests that Luke 24 (especially verse 49 onwards) is intended as a highly condensed account of what happened. Given that, the various accounts are compatible with initial appearances to disciples in the Jerusalem area; then one or more appearances to disciples in Galilee (where many of Jesus's disciples were presumably to be found, and so the appearance to 'more than five hundred brothers and sisters at one time' would have taken place); and then one or more final appearances to the Twelve, who were told to return to Jerusalem in order to begin their missionary work from there.

So I think that there is no difficulty in resolving the major apparent differences between the sources about who saw Jesus where. Minor differences are to be expected for the general reason given in the previous chapter: the fading of memories and difficulty of communication between different historians.

Paul would not have given the Corinthians the list of witnesses which he did unless Peter and James (with whom he spent fifteen days three years after his conversion) and the other people who had known the Apostles and others involved in the Easter events had confirmed that the people listed did indeed see Jesus in roughly the order given. As I claimed in the previous chapter, Paul comes over as an honest witness, and we must take his word for what the Twelve and others were claiming about the appearances of the risen Jesus. Many of the Twelve and other **early Christians** died rather than recant their beliefs. So they **were not seeking to deceive us.** The only possibility, other than that what they said was true, was that they were themselves deceived in some way. While individuals might imagine that Jesus appeared to them and even that they had a conversation with him, some of these appearances involve several people together having conversations with Jesus of some length. It is **massively improbable that there could be such joint illusions of detailed conversations.**

The Empty Tomb

And then there is the empty tomb. All four Gospels begin their accounts of the Resurrection with the visit on the first Easter Sunday morning by women to the tomb, which they found empty. (All the Gospels also claim that the women reported that they were greeted there by one or two 'young men in white' or 'angels' who told them that Jesus was risen.) It has often been said that, as 1 **Corinthians,** the earliest source, **does not mention the empty tomb,** this visit and the tomb being empty must have been later inventions of the Gospel writers in order to give further support to their belief in the Resurrection, which was based solely on the appearances of Jesus. But if the Gospel writers felt this need, presumably it was because they felt that appearances of a ghost of Jesus were not nearly as worth having as appearances of Jesus embodied. Luke's claim that Jesus ate fish in front of them (Luke 24: 37–43) to demonstrate that he was no ghost shows that an embodied Jesus alone would not have given them the joy of the Resurrection. And although Jesus might have been embodied in a new body, this was not a possibility that would readily have occurred to first-century Jews; they would have expected his embodiment to go with an empty tomb.

But if the Gospel writers felt that a resurrection required an empty tomb, presumably Christians of a decade or two earlier would have felt the same; St Paul would have felt that. So if there was a belief held by anyone in the Church or outside it that the body of Jesus still lay in its tomb, surely Paul would have felt the need either to deny that the body was still in the tomb or to explain how really the fact that the body was still in the tomb made no difference to Resurrection faith. Those whom he is addressing in 1 Corinthians who held that 'there is no resurrection of the dead' would have had an argument to support them—even the body of Jesus was still in the tomb—which would need to be answered. But 1 Corinthians shows no awareness of any such objection, nor does any other New Testament book. It was part of the tradition that Paul mentions, that immediately precedes the claim that Jesus 'was raised', that Jesus 'was buried'. Peter's first sermon recorded in Acts contrasts the patriarch David, who was also buried, 'and his tomb is with us to this day', with David's prophecy, which Peter interprets as referring to Jesus, that 'his flesh' did not 'experience corruption' (Acts 2: 29–31). And even the Jews acknowledged that the tomb was empty. For Matthew 28: 15 records that the Jews claimed that the disciples had stolen the body, which they would not have claimed if they did not believe that the tomb was empty. **Why Paul didn't mention the empty tomb is because he didn't need to.** Resurrection for a Jew meant bodily resurrection.

And there is one crucial largely unrecognized piece of evidence in favour of the women having visited the tomb on the first Easter Day and having found it empty. Christian communities spread out from Jerusalem very quickly—within three or four years of the events of the Passion. They took with them their customs, including the custom of celebrating a eucharist; and all the evidence we have suggests that there was a **universal custom of celebrating the eucharist on a Sunday**, the first day of the week. This must have pre-dated the 'spread'; otherwise we would have heard of disputes about when to celebrate, and some instructions being given from on high (analogous to the way in which disputes about circumcision and eating sacrificial meat were resolved by the 'Council of Jerusalem' described in Acts 15). All references in early Christian literature to when the eucharist was celebrated refer to a weekly Sunday celebration. And the one apparent explicit reference in the New Testament to a particular post-Ascension celebration of the eucharist (Acts 20: 7) records a 'breaking of bread' on a 'first day of the week'. ('To break bread' was the expression used by St Paul in 1 Corinthians for what Jesus did at the Last Supper, and was always used later as a description of the common Christian meal which included the eucharist.) This verse is one of the 'we' passages in Acts (see p. 93). 1 Corinthians 16: 2 implies that Christian communities met together on Sundays; and Revelation 1: 10 calls Sunday 'the Lord's day'.

There are other days on which it might have been more natural for Christians to celebrate the eucharist (e.g. on the day of the original Last Supper, a Thursday; or annually rather than weekly). No such customs are known. There is no plausible origin of the sacredness of Sunday from outside Christianity. There is only one simple explanation of this universal custom, which, I argued, must derive at the latest from the first two or three post-Resurrection years. The eucharist was celebrated on a Sunday (and Sunday had theological significance) from the first years of Christianity because Christians believed that the central Christian event of the Resurrection occurred on a Sunday. Yet such early practice would have included that of the Twelve themselves, and so could only go with a belief of theirs that Christians had seen either the empty tomb or the risen Jesus on the first Easter Sunday (and in the latter case, they would certainly have checked out the tomb then). This shows that the visit to the tomb on Easter Sunday was not a late invention read back into history to make sense of the appearances but a separately authenticated incident.

One reason why scholars have believed that the visit to the tomb on the Sunday morning was a late Christian invention is that when the early Christians searched the Old Testament to find predictions of the Resurrection they discovered the **prophecy of Hosea** (6: 2) spoken originally about the nation of Israel, 'After two days he will revive us: on the third day he will raise us up.' So, these scholars claimed, that must have led Christians to read back into history the story of the visit of the women on 'the third day', which is the Sunday after the Friday Crucifixion. However, although there are two passages in the New Testament which claim that 'the third day' is an Old Testament prediction, the passage from Hosea is never cited. The one passage from the Old Testament which is cited as an Old Testament prediction of the length of time for which Jesus would remain in the tomb is a sentence from the book of Jonah. Matthew's Gospel (12: 40) claims that Jesus said, 'As Jonah was three days and three nights in the belly of the sea monster, so for three days and three nights the Son of Man will be in the heart of the earth.' But this citation doesn't make the comparison Matthew needs. Matthew believed that Jesus rose on a Sunday after only two nights 'in the heart of the earth'. If **Matthew** put such an inaccurate text about the length of time which Jesus would spend in the tomb into the mouth of Jesus, that shows that he **first**

believed that Jesus was raised on the Sunday and then did his best to find a near-prediction of it in the Old Testament, rather than fitting his account of the facts to the prediction. And that in turn suggests, as does the evidence of the Sunday celebration of the eucharist, that the tradition of the visit by the women to the tomb on the Sunday morning was a very early tradition indeed.

The Unexpectedness of the Resurrection

The Resurrection, like other features of the life and death of Jesus, was unexpected. To cite again the Jewish scholar Geza Vermes, '[Jesus's] disciples did not expect him to arise from the dead any more than their contemporaries expected the Messiah to do so' (*Jesus the Jew*, SCM Press, 1994, 20). It may or may not be the case that, as Mark (and Matthew and Luke) claim, Jesus predicted his Passion and his Resurrection; but if so, the prediction of the Resurrection fell on deaf ears. The women went to the tomb to anoint the body of Jesus, not to check whether he was risen. The message of the angels at the tomb was good news, and, all the accounts agree, highly unexpected. The disciples at first did not believe the women's report: their words appeared as 'an idle tale and they did not believe them' (Luke 24: 11); and they still 'were disbelieving in their joy' (Luke 24: 41) when, it seemed to them, they saw Jesus. John tells how Thomas did not believe that the 'other disciples' had seen Jesus; and in this story Thomas may represent further disciples as well. The 'Marcan appendix' (Mark 16: 9–20) reports similar disbelief. Although subsequently the disciples came to believe that the Resurrection not merely occurred but had significance and had been predicted (they thought) by the Old Testament, they had not understood the Old Testament to make such a prediction before it happened. Jesus needed to explain these things when, according to Luke, he had the long talk with two disciples on the road to Emmaus (Luke 24: 13–32). 'Oh, how foolish you are and slow of heart to believe all that prophets have declared,' was the rebuke of Jesus to the disciples who expressed their amazement at the empty tomb. 'Was it not necessary that the Messiah should suffer these things and then enter into his glory? Then beginning with Moses and all the prophets he interpreted to them the things about himself in all the Scriptures.' And speaking afterwards to the Eleven, Jesus claimed to have done this explaining before the Crucifixion; but he went on to do it again: 'Then he opened their minds to understand the Scriptures; and he said to them, "Thus it is written that the Messiah is to suffer and rise from the dead on the third day."' John also comments that, when the disciples saw the empty tomb, 'as yet they did not understand the Scripture, that he must rise from the dead'. The unanimity of all the accounts on this point powerfully indicates that **the disciples did not force themselves to believe in the Resurrection because they expected it**.

If Jesus did not rise from the dead, what happened to his body?

There are five possible theories, but they **all have massive difficulties**. First, there is the theory that Jesus was not dead when he was taken down from the Cross, and recovered in the cool of the tomb. But he could hardly have recovered enough to escape from his burial cloth, push away the stone from the tomb, convince his followers not merely that he was alive but in supernatural health, able to vanish and pass through doors etc (as Luke 24: 31 and John 20: 19 and 26 claim). And what happened to him after the 'appearances'? It seems very unlikely that he would have gone to live in some remote non-Jewish village and taken no further interest in his movement. Secondly, there is the theory that the body remained in the tomb but his disciples mistook an empty tomb for the tomb of Jesus. But Joseph of Arimathea, who owned the tomb, would soon have spotted the mistake; and if for some reason he didn't, the Jewish leaders would soon have checked out whether the tomb in which Jesus was buried was really empty when the Christian movement began to claim (as it did very soon) that Jesus had risen. And then there are theories that the body was stolen—either by enemies of Jesus (to prevent it from becoming the centre of a cult), or by grave-robbers, or by Jesus's disciples (as the Jewish leaders claimed). If the enemies of Jesus had stolen the body, they would have produced that body when the Christian movement took off in order to disprove its central claim (or at least the robbers would have identified themselves to the Jewish leaders in the reasonable hope of being rewarded for this information). Grave-robbers were not interested in bodies, only in valuables put in graves. Jews did not normally bury valuables in graves, but if they had done so on this occasion, it would have been these and not the body that grave-robbers would have stolen. None of the last three theories as such accounts for the 'appearances', for which a separate account would be needed. And if the body had been stolen by friends of Jesus, they would have told his other friends in order that they might share in devotion to the body. But that involves claiming not merely that there were no 'appearances', but also massive deceit by the whole Christian movement in their accounts of the appearances, which—as I wrote before—is extremely implausible in view of the readiness of the first Christian leaders to die for their faith. Of course, sceptics can provide further hypotheses to account for these objections, but only at the cost of making the sceptical theories very complicated and so very improbable.

The Resurrection as God's Signature

The bodily Resurrection of Jesus (if it occurred) would be manifestly not merely a violation of natural laws, requiring the action (or permission) of God to bring it about, but the kind of miracle which could be recognized by his Jewish contemporaries as God's authenticating signature on the life of Jesus. It would show it to have fulfilled the purposes which I have described, and contemporary Christians claimed that it did show just that.

The Old Testament had two criteria for a prophet being a **genuine prophet.** The first is that he must teach in the name of the Lord God, and not try to divert people to the worship of other gods. Deuteronomy (13: 1–3) claims that, if prophets say 'follow other gods' and promise 'omens or portents' as evidence of the genuineness of their message, then—even if these 'omens or portents' occur—'you must not heed the words of those prophets'. And, of course, Jesus fulfilled this criterion. He spoke in the name of the Lord God and told the Jews to worship that God, the God of Israel. The second criterion was that, if the prophet makes a prophecy about the future, it must come to pass: 'If a prophet speaks in the name of the Lord, but the thing does not take place or prove true, it is a word that the Lord has not spoken. The prophet has spoken it presumptuously; do not be frightened by it' (Deuteronomy 18: 22). The 'thing' must presumably not be one that might be expected to occur in the ordinary cause of nature; and clearly the more evidently miraculous the 'thing', the more it showed. A miracle in response to a prayer from the prophet to show that he was a true prophet would clearly also fulfil this criterion, and abundantly well. This is shown by the story of Elijah and the prophets of Baal. Elijah called on God to provide fire from Heaven to ignite a water-sodden sacrifice (1 Kings 18: 17–40), which involves doing an act which (in the view of his contemporaries and expressed in my terminology) would violate laws of nature. When the fire came from Heaven, it led to the recognition by Israel that Elijah was a true prophet, and the elimination of the prophets of Baal. (I am not arguing here that this story is true. I am using it merely to illustrate ancient Israel's criteria for true prophecy.) The future event, especially an obviously miraculous event, would constitute God's signature on the work of the prophet.

The Jews of the time of Jesus were very familiar with this understanding of what would constitute God's signature on the work of a prophet. The verse from Deuteronomy which I have just quoted occurs at the end of a section in which Moses declares to Israel that 'the Lord your God will raise up for you a prophet like me from among your own people; you shall heed such a prophet'. The latter verse was one which, according to the reports in Acts of their sermons in the first year or two after the Crucifixion, both Peter and Stephen quote and which Peter saw as referring to Jesus. So if the Resurrection occurred as described, it would certainly constitute God's signature on the work of Jesus on the Jewish understanding of a signature—if Jesus had predicted it.

Did Jesus predict the Resurrection? Mark's Gospel tells us that he predicted both his Passion and Resurrection explicitly on three separate occasions. But putting explicit predictions of the subsequent fate of heroes into their mouths or the mouths of others was a habit of ancient writers; and so many modern critics doubt whether Jesus really made these predictions. Nevertheless, although they may not have mentioned a bodily resurrection after three days, **three important predictions** which Jesus did make **were fulfilled** (in whole or part) **by his Resurrection**. The first is his claim that he would provide the sacrifice of his own life to make atonement for our sins; I argued in the previous chapter that Jesus did make this claim. A sacrifice to God only provides atonement if it is accepted by God. So Jesus was predicting that God (the Father) would accept the sacrifice. As I commented in Chapter 4, on the way of thinking lying behind the Old Testament, the sacrifice (in the form of its smoke) had to reach God himself, who would often return some of it to the worshippers by allowing them to eat some of the flesh of the sacrificed animal. The Letter to the Hebrews claims that **Jesus's sacrifice achieved its goal**, when Jesus entered not into 'a sanctuary made by human hands', but 'into Heaven itself, now to appear in the presence of God on our behalf' (Hebrews 9: 24). So Jesus's exaltation was necessary for completion of the sacrifice. We see that Jesus has been exalted because the 'God of peace . . . brought back from the dead our Lord Jesus, the great shepherd of the sheep, by the blood of the eternal covenant' (Hebrews 13: 20). The Resurrection shows that Jesus is exalted, no doubt in virtue of the superhuman powers which he then manifested, and by his not dying again but ceasing to live on earth. Hence, it fulfilled the prediction of Jesus that his sacrifice would be accepted by God.

Secondly, the Resurrection provided a **partial fulfilment of Jesus's prediction that all humans would be raised from the dead** by showing that one human (Jesus) was raised. That showed that resurrection is possible, and so could happen to us.

And thirdly, the Resurrection of Jesus was a resurrection in which **Jesus had supernatural powers** (to pass through doors etc.). I argued in the previous chapter that Jesus did claim a divine status. In coming to life again with supernatural powers, Jesus would at least be showing that he had a supernatural status, and that is some of the way towards showing his divinity.

The Creed claims that Jesus 'rose again on the third day, **in accordance with the Scriptures**'; and, as I noted earlier, Luke's Gospel claims that after his Resurrection Jesus himself explained to his disciples how both his suffering and his 'entering into glory' were predicted by 'the prophets', that is, in the Old Testament. There are some few Old Testament passages which seem to predict an ultimate glorious victory after suffering leading to apparent failure that have an uncanny resemblance to the details of the Gospel accounts of the Passion and Resurrection of Jesus. The most obvious ones are the 'Suffering Servant' passages in Isaiah (especially chapter 53) and some of the Psalms (especially Psalm 22). And in a more general sense, if what I have claimed in previous chapters is true, Jesus 'fulfilled' the Old Testament in providing many things for which so many writers of the Old Testament (at various stages of its production) longed: adequate atonement for sins, the triumph of good over evil, and a deep understanding (a 'vision') of God. And he was going on to provide a Church designed to convert the whole world (for which later Old Testament books such as the book of Jonah longed), and the bodily resurrection of all good humans (which only the very latest books of the Old Testament affirmed).

The Prior Probability of the Resurrection

If we knew that there was no God, we would know that the laws of nature are the ultimate determinants of what happens; and so that there cannot be a violation of a law of nature and so the Resurrection cannot have occurred. But if there is at least a moderate probability that there is a God, then there is a moderate probability that there is someone able to violate the laws of nature with reason occasionally to do so, and in particular to do so in order to put his signature on the life of God Incarnate. There is, then, already a moderate prior probability that there would be an event such as the Resurrection which would put God's signature on the life of a prophet whose life and teaching were of the right kind. There is evidence about the life and teaching of Jesus, described in Chapter 7, of a kind to be expected (that is, which it is quite probable we would find) if Jesus was that prophet (and not to be expected of Jesus otherwise). So that gives us reason, in advance of looking at the historical evidence for the Resurrection, for expecting that God would put his signature on the work of Jesus and so that an event like the Resurrection would occur. That is, there is a **prior probability** (before it occurred) **that the Resurrection would occur** much greater than there would be if the prior probability of the existence of God was much less than I have supposed. So, although we certainly need historical evidence (in the form of various kinds of witness testimony) in order to make it probable that the Resurrection occurred, we don't need nearly as much of it as we would if we had little reason to believe that there is a God or that the life and teaching of Jesus were of the right kind.

That the amount of witness testimony we need in order to believe what witnesses tell us depends on the prior probability of what they claim to have observed can be seen from a simple **analogy**. We know that almost all men are less than 7 feet tall; we have never seen and no witness whom other evidence shows to be mildly trustworthy reports having seen a man more than 12 feet tall. So on that evidence it is immensely improbable that there is a man 15 feet tall. If I told you that I had seen a man 15 feet tall, you would be right to disbelieve me; my testimony by itself would not be enough to make it probable that there is such a man. But if I told you that I had seen a man who was 10 feet tall, it would (if there was no reason to suppose that I am lying or have bad eyesight) be right to believe me. This is because, although the prior probability that I would see a man who is 10 feet tall is fairly small, it is not very small. So it is plausible (in my sense of 'not very improbable') that I would see such a man. Hence, in virtue of the Principle of Testimony, my having told you that I had seen a man 10 feet tall would give you enough evidence to make it probable that I had done so; whereas you would need, as well as my testimony, the testimony of several different witnesses on different occasions that they had seen men 13 or 14 feet tall if testimony is to make it at all probable that I have seen a man 15 feet tall. So, if there is a modest prior probability that there is a God and evidence to be expected if Jesus had lived the right kind of life (and not to be expected otherwise), and no evidence that any other prophet had lived the right kind of life, **we don't need too much witness testimony to make it probable that Jesus rose from the dead**. There are a lot of witnesses of the empty tomb and of conversations between Jesus and several other people of some length, whom, for the reasons which I have given, there is good reason to regard as trustworthy witnesses. I conclude that **there is significant historical evidence of a kind which it is quite probable we would have if Jesus rose from the dead** (and very improbable we would have if he did not rise from the dead), and so significant evidence of the occurrence of an event which would constitute God's signature on the work of Jesus and so God's endorsement of the teaching of Jesus.

9 PROVISIONAL CONCLUSION

I argued in Part I that we would expect God (if there is a God) to become a human prophet and lead the kind of life and give the kind of teaching considered in Chapter 7, and to put his signature on that life by a miraculous event, such as a resurrection of that human prophet from the dead. I argued in Chapter 7 that there is significant evidence that Jesus led the kind of life and gave the kind of teaching which we would expect God Incarnate to live and give; and I argued in Chapter 8 that (given the existence of God and the life and teaching of Jesus) that there is significant evidence that Jesus rose from the dead, and that his Resurrection constituted God's signature on his life and teaching. But just how significant is 'significant'? It will, I hope, be useful to assess at this stage how probable these two sets of evidence make the claim that Jesus was God Incarnate, before I take into account the other evidence which, I claimed in Part I, is relevant to our topic—whether the later Church gave plausible interpretations of Jesus's teaching.

How to Assess the Probability that Jesus Was God

It is **not possible** (except in a few cases) **to give precise numerical values** to any probabilities of actual occurrences or scientific hypotheses, or to any of the terms involved in the calculation of the probability of any scientific or historical hypothesis. All one can say in the vast majority of cases is that the probability of a certain event or hypothesis is high, or that it is very low, or that it is greater than the probability of some other hypothesis, or 'plausible' (which I am using in the sense of 'not very improbable') or something of this sort. But in order to show clearly that some hypothesis or event is moderately probable (or whatever) or to show what follows from that, it is sometimes necessary to replace such vague expressions by artificially precise numerical values within the range covered by the vague expressions. Probability is measured between 1 and 0.

A hypothesis that has a probability of 1 is certainly true, a hypothesis that has a probability of 0 is certainly false, a hypothesis that has a probability of $\frac{1}{2}$ is as probable as not (that is, as likely to be true as to be false), and so on. And by 'moderately probable' I'll mean having a probability of about $\frac{1}{4}$, by 'quite probable' having a probability of about $\frac{2}{5}$, by 'very probable' having a probability of about $\frac{3}{4}$, and by 'very probable indeed' having a probability a bit greater than that.

Probability theory tells us that if some hypothesis has a certain prior probability and **if it is a lot more probable that we would have such and such evidence if the hypothesis were true than we would if the hypothesis were false, then that evidence makes the hypothesis a lot more probable than its prior probability.** Take the example of the burglary set out in Chapter 1. Suppose that on the evidence of John's previous behaviour there is a prior probability of $\frac{1}{4}$ that he would commit the particular burglary, and that it is a lot more probable that we would find the new evidence we do if he committed the burglary than if he did not commit the burglary. We saw that we might expect to find his fingerprints on the safe etc. if John did commit the burglary, a lot more than if he didn't. Then that makes the hypothesis that John committed the burglary a lot more probable. If for example, it is twice as probable that we would have the evidence we do if that hypothesis is true than if it is false, then that makes the hypothesis somewhat less than twice as probable as it was. (The exact value of the 'somewhat less' depends on the numerical difference between the probability of the evidence if the hypothesis is true and its probability if the hypothesis is false.)

I outlined in Chapter 1 the considerations relevant to ascribing a prior probability to the existence of God. We must come to the issue of the truth of Christian doctrines with a view about this. So let us suppose that there is a moderate prior probability that there is a God (as expounded in Chapter 1). And to give it an artificially precise numerical value, I am going to understand by that a probability of $\frac{1}{4}$. (Some proposition has a probability of $\frac{1}{4}$ if it is three times more probable that it is false than that it is true.) If my arguments in Part I are cogent, the existence of God entails that (if humans suffer a lot, as they do) he will become incarnate, live a life including much suffering, claim to be God Incarnate, found a Church to continue his work, and his life will be culminated by a miracle such as the Resurrection; and it makes it quite probable that that life will be a perfect life, that he will claim to be making atonement for our sins, and that he will give us plausible moral and theological teaching.

The Only Candidate

The reasons which I set out in Part I for expecting that God would become incarnate and live a certain sort of perfect life on which he would put his signature were **reasons merely for expecting one incarnation** of that kind. Although God might choose to become incarnate more than once, the need for an incarnation in order to show solidarity with our suffering, provide atonement for our wrongdoing, and reveal truths to us could be satisfied by one incarnation of that kind. For example, by living one perfect human life on earth, he would have shown solidarity with the suffering of each ordinary human who lives only one life on earth. So if our evidence about the life of Jesus is to be strong evidence that he was God Incarnate, it needs to be the case that he is the only serious candidate in human history about whom we have evidence that he lived the right kind of life ending with a divine signature. He must be the **only founder of a religion or other prophet about whom there is good historical evidence that his or her life had the requisite character** (that is, evidence that it had most of the features discussed in Chapter 7 possessed by the life of Jesus) **and ended with a divine signature** (such as the Resurrection). This requirement is easily satisfied. Whatever the quality of the life and teaching of Muhammad or Moses, they certainly made no claims to be God Incarnate or to be making atonement for human sins. Nor did the Buddha, who did not believe in a personal God of the kind for which, I am assuming, there is significant evidence. And although many modern messiahs have claimed to be God Incarnate, there is no evidence of the perfection of their lives or of much suffering in them. And it is also the case that there is no other founder of a major religion or other prophet about whom there is evidence of anything like the strength that there is about the Resurrection of Jesus, that his or her life ended with such a miracle. Islam has not claimed this for Muhammad, nor has Buddhism claimed it for the Buddha. And while other religions have put forward claims of miraculous foundation events, there is not for such events the strength of evidence that there is for the Resurrection of Jesus. So if there is a God and so God would become incarnate (as I have argued that he would), and this incarnation has already happened, it was very clearly in Jesus that he became incarnate.

But what about the possibility **that Jesus was not God Incarnate, but that God will become incarnate at some future time?** There are two reasons why this 'possibility' **is an extremely improbable** one. First, I suggest that it would have been dishonest of God to allow the occurrence of evidence of the strength that there is with respect to Jesus that he was God Incarnate if he was not in fact God Incarnate. Secondly, the evidence with respect to a future prophet would have to be evidence of the same kind but very much stronger if it was to convince us that it was the future prophet and not Jesus who was God Incarnate. If the evidence was only a bit stronger, it would be unclear which prophet was God Incarnate. To make it clear that the new prophet was God Incarnate, there would have to be TV cameras watching his (or her) resurrection etc. Yet such overwhelming evidence that God had intervened in human history, and so that there is a God concerned for our future, would not merely help people to live God-directed lives; it would make it very obvious that it was in their own selfish interest to do so (if they were to avoid being deprived of Heaven). While we need it to be quite probable that there is a God and so that it would be good to live a certain kind of life (including, for example, worshipping God, and dealing with our wrongdoing in a certain way), we need a serious choice of whether or not to pursue what is probably the right way of life or to neglect to do so. Only with some uncertainty about whether God had become incarnate, and so about whether there is a God and so about how it is good to live, can we show any serious dedication to the good by pursuing what is probably the right way to live when we may be mistaken. What we can learn from the fact of suffering, I suggested in Chapter 1, is that, if there is a God, he wants us to choose the sort of people we are to be. It would be much less easy to do that if he provided overwhelming evidence about some prophet that that prophet was God Incarnate. I conclude that, if there is a God, he became incarnate in Jesus.

It is not merely the case that Jesus is the only serious candidate in human history about whom we have evidence that he lived the right kind of life which ended with a divine signature. **Jesus was both the only prophet in human history about whose life there is good historical evidence of the first kind** (evidence that he or she lived a perfect life with much suffering, claimed to be divine, claimed to be making atonement, gave plausible moral and theological teaching, and founded a Church to continue his work), **and also the only prophet about whose life there is good historical evidence of the second kind** (evidence that his or her life ended with a miracle recognizable as a divine signature). Not merely did Muhammad or the Buddha not give the right sort of teaching (they did not claim to be God Incarnate etc.), but their lives ended in altogether non-miraculous ways. And similarly for all other great prophets about whom we have evidence. (And if there are prophets about whom we don't have evidence, we cannot take seriously their claims to be God Incarnate providing good news for all humanity.) This shows that the **coincidence of the two sets of evidence** about one prophet that his or her life exhibited both features would be very improbable in the normal course of things. It would be **very improbable unless God arranged it**. And, as mentioned above, it would have been dishonest of God to arrange evidence of this kind unless that prophet was indeed God Incarnate. And in virtue of his perfect goodness God would not do that. Hence the **coincidence of the two kinds of evidence** does not merely make it very probable that, if there is a God, he became incarnate in Jesus, but it **makes it much more probable than it would be otherwise that there is a God**. If there is already a prior probability of $\frac{1}{4}$ that there is a God, the posterior probability of this, given historical evidence quite probable if there is a God and very improbable otherwise, will be much greater than $\frac{1}{2}$. And so, since it is very probable indeed that if there is a God he became incarnate in Jesus, it is very probable that there is a God who became incarnate in Jesus.

We can see this from **another analogy**. Suppose we already have evidence which makes it moderately probable that a Ruritanian secret agent has arrived in our country. We know that, if there is such an agent, there are two things which he will (quite probably) try to do: kill several well-known Ruritanian dissidents, and buy spare parts for Ruritanian fighter aeroplanes (parts which our laws forbid us to export). The available evidence strongly suggests that there have never been any previous attempts to kill these dissidents nor any previous attempts to buy spare parts for these particular aeroplanes. We now acquire new evidence both that these dissidents have eaten poisoned food after having a meal with a mysterious foreigner, and that an employee of the aeroplane manufacturer reports to the police that someone looking like that foreigner has been trying to bribe him to send spare parts to Ruritania. These two pieces of evidence are such as are to be expected if there is a Ruritanian secret agent in the country. But it is most improbable that, when there have never been any previous attempts to kill these dissidents or to buy parts for these aeroplanes, there should suddenly be evidence of both types of attempt at the same time—by mere coincidence. Hence not merely does the new evidence make it very probable that, if there is a Ruritanian agent in the country, he is trying to kill the dissidents and buy spare parts, but it makes it very probable indeed that there is a Ruritanian agent in the country, and very probable that there is an agent who is trying to kill dissidents and buy spare parts.

So my provisional conclusion is that if there is a moderate prior probability on other evidence that there is a God, it becomes very probable indeed when the historical evidence discussed in Chapters 7 and 8 is added, and so very probable on the total evidence that Jesus was God Incarnate. It will also be apparent that, even if the prior probability of the existence of God is quite a bit less than $\frac{1}{4}$, the historical evidence will still make it more probable than not that Jesus was God Incarnate.

10 THE CHURCH

The Identity of the Church

I have argued that, on the evidence of the life of Jesus, if it is already moderately probable that there is a God, it is very probable that Jesus was God Incarnate. But there was one further requirement which, I claimed in Part I, a prophet's life would need to satisfy if it was to be the life of God Incarnate, and that is that the Church which he founded should give plausible interpretations of his teaching—ones both plausible as interpretations and whose content is plausibly true. God would need to ensure that the Church did this; otherwise the work and teaching of God Incarnate, which he needed to make available to all humanity, would not be available to them. Any human society without some divine help could so easily misinterpret its founder's actions and teaching in implausible ways. I did not discuss in Chapter 7 whether our evidence is such as would be expected if this requirement was satisfied by the Church which Jesus founded, as I wished to complete my historical discussion of the life and immediately subsequent history of Jesus by considering in Chapter 8 the evidence for his Resurrection. But we must now consider whether the subsequent Church interpreted the life and teaching of Jesus in the right way.

Only when the work of Jesus on earth was finished could there be any authoritative statement about the whole of his life and its significance; and this would have to be provided by the **Apostolic Church** (in the sense of the Church of the Apostles as it existed immediately after the (believed) Resurrection of Jesus). When, as I mentioned earlier, some twenty years after the end of Jesus's life, a decision was taken by a council of 'Apostles and elders' (Acts 15: 6) that there was no need any more to conform to the Old Testament laws of ritual and sacrifice, they recorded their decision in a general letter reporting that 'it has seemed good to the Holy Spirit and to us' to make this decision. So they regarded themselves as filling out, and not merely interpreting, the teaching of Jesus—as I have argued that they should so regard themselves. The later Church considered that revelation ended with the death of the last of the twelve Apostles; after that all that the Church could do is to draw out the implications of what had already been revealed and apply it to new circumstances.

So if the Resurrection is to be regarded (as I am arguing) as God's signature on the teaching of Jesus, it must also be regarded as God's signature on the teaching of the Apostolic Church about Jesus and the implications of his work. But if the teaching of Jesus and so the benefits of his life, death, and Resurrection were to become available to new cultures and generations, this Church has to continue. So **we need evidence that the Apostolic Church founded by Jesus has continued until today and that it provides a plausible account of his actions and teaching and that of the Apostolic Church, and plausible interpretations thereof which are plausibly true**. By 'plausible' I repeat that I mean 'not very improbable'. It may be that there is an equally plausible rival (account or) interpretation of some of Jesus's actions or teaching to one given by the later Church. Yet the fact that the later Church taught a certain plausible interpretation will, in view of the evidence for its divinely authenticated status, be evidence that that is the true interpretation. (The evidence for its divinely authenticated status is that it was founded by Jesus, whose divine authority was shown by all the evidence set out in Chapters 7 and 8; and that without God's continuing guidance of the interpretations provided by that Church, the incarnation would have lost its point.) But if the later Church taught an interpretation which is quite implausible, that is evidence against its divine status and so against the whole body of Christian doctrine.

Ever since its foundation the Church has been subject to divisions about the content of Christian doctrine and about the way the Church should be organized; and these divisions have often led to formal separations, 'schisms', resulting in the creation of two or more separately organized 'churches' which I'll call '**ecclesial bodies**'. While many such ecclesial bodies have ceased to exist, or have joined up with others, there are today five or six main ecclesial bodies (or groups thereof): Roman Catholics, Orthodox, monophysites (Copts and other Middle Eastern groups in communion with each other), 'Nestorians' (the Church of the East, a small Middle Eastern group), Anglicans, and many groups of Protestants.

So which, if any, of the ecclesial bodies is the Church founded by Jesus, or do they all together (despite their divisions) constitute that Church?

What makes a society (a club or a university, for example) **at one time the same society as some society at an earlier time?** There are, I suggest, two criteria: continuity of aim and continuity of organization. By **continuity of aim** I mean having a similar aim to the original society, any differences arising from a gradual development over the intervening time. Suppose that a football club was founded in 1850; it ceased to play football in 1900, but its members continued to meet and formed themselves into a political party. That party would not be the same society as the original football club because the society no longer had to any extent the same aim. But if it continued to play football but with somewhat different rules, that wouldn't be enough to make it a different society. By **continuity of organization** I mean having a similar organization to the original society, any differences arising from a gradual development over the intervening time. New members have to be admitted, new officers elected with similar powers in accord with procedures similar to the original procedures (and if there is a written constitution, more or less in a way laid down in that constitution). If the football club went bankrupt and its members ceased to meet but other men came together and formed a club to play football on the same ground, they would not constitute the same society.

In the case of the Church, **continuity of aim amounts to continuity of doctrine**. The Church's aim is for its members to live and worship in a certain way, and to persuade others to join them in this; and that way is determined by the Church's teachings about how to live and worship, and so by its doctrines about what God is like and how he wants us to live. So to be a later part of the Apostolic Church which Jesus founded, an ecclesial body must teach what Jesus did and taught and what the Apostolic Church taught about what Jesus did, or rather—given the need for interpretation on which I commented in Chapter 5—plausible interpretations of the teaching of Jesus and the Apostolic Church.

Some claims to be part of the Church can be ruled out on the grounds that the doctrines taught by some body are not plausible interpretations of the teaching of Jesus and the Apostolic Church. Some body which advocated polygamy or taught pantheism (that everything was divine) would have doctrines evidently quite contrary to the teaching not merely of Jesus (about which that body might argue that we had been deceived) but of all ecclesial bodies which had any continuity of doctrine with the Apostolic Church.

But **sometimes**, as I shall emphasize shortly, **it is not obvious which of two conflicting doctrines follows most plausibly from the teaching of Jesus**, and so which ecclesial body satisfies this criterion best. So in order to resolve questions about whether some ecclesial body is part of the Church, it is important to have also the other criterion: the criterion of continuity of organization. An ecclesial body having continuity of organization with the Apostolic Church involves its members being admitted in a similar way (by baptism) and its leaders being commissioned with similar powers in similar ways (by ordination) to those of earlier leaders, and so on back to the Apostolic Church, any differences arising only from gradual development. It also involves having similar procedures for determining which interpretations of doctrine (among those which are plausible candidates for satisfying the test of continuity of doctrine) are the correct ones.

When a society splits into two societies, it is **sometimes** the case that **each of the subsequent societies has greater continuity with the original society in a different respect**. Suppose a football club votes in accord with its constitution in future to play rugby football instead of soccer, but a minority breaks away and continues to play soccer. The majority may claim greater continuity of organization with the original club, while the minority may claim greater continuity of aim. Where there are two more or less equally good candidates for being the same society as an original society, what we must say, surely, is that the society is split. Only both groups together could constitute the original society.

Schisms are produced both by **disagreements about the inter-pretation of doctrine**, and by **disagreements about whether Church officers have been properly commissioned** and about what their powers are. The fourth-century schism between the Catholics (a term used then in a much wider sense than the later Roman Catholics), who claimed that the Son (Jesus) was 'of the same substance' as the Father (that is, fully divine), and the Arians, who claimed that the Son was 'of similar substance' to the Father (that is, almost divine), was a division solely about doctrine. The eleventh-century schism between Roman Catholics and Orthodox was largely concerned with organization. Both agreed that bishops were the Church leaders and they had to be ordained by other bishops. Roman Catholics, however, insisted that the Pope, the bishop of Rome, had great authority over all Christians, while the Orthodox denied this. Roman Catholics came to insist that, while the natural method of resolving doctrinal differences was by a vote of an 'Ecumenical Council' of bishops (who recognized the Pope's authority) from all parts of the Church, the Pope acting alone had authority to resolve these differences. Later Roman Catholics came to insist that a Pope acting alone could issue a doctrinal definition which (unlike most of his doctrinal pronouncements) was infallible (that is, necessarily true, quite incapable of being amended by later decisions). The Orthodox, however, claimed that only an Ecumenical Council of bishops (and not only ones who recognized the Pope's authority) could decide issues of doctrine infallibly; and that the Pope's approval of a doctrinal decision of an Ecumenical Council was not needed in order to give it infallible authority. And many Orthodox claim that a council is only an 'Ecumenical' council if there is subsequently a widespread recognition in the Church that its decisions are correct.

The sixteenth-century schism between Roman Catholics and Protestants (and Anglicans) turned both on issues of doctrine and on issues of organization. Most Protestants put forward doctrines about human nature which contradicted more 'liberal' Roman Catholic (and Orthodox) doctrines. Protestants emphasized (to varying degrees) the depths of original sin and our guilt for it, and the inability of humans to reform themselves, asserting that we could only be saved by a faith in God given to us by God. Roman Catholics claimed that human free will was not totally damaged by original sin, and that humans need to do more than just believe in God in order to achieve salvation. The differences also turned on organization: the Protestant bodies (but not the Anglicans) claimed that the Church leaders need not be bishops ordained by earlier bishops; they might be ordained by priests or simply by congregations of the baptized. And all Protestants (and most Anglicans) claimed that the only way to resolve doctrinal differences was by deriving doctrines directly from the Bible, independently of any previous Church decisions of councils or Pope.

Despite these differences between Protestants and other Christians, for the past thousand years **almost all ecclesial bodies** (at least until the last fifty years) **satisfied the criterion of continuity of doctrine** to a very large extent. Like the others, as I mentioned in Chapter 1, almost all Protestants in effect accepted the Nicene Creed. They also shared the common Christian moral teaching which I mentioned in Chapter 5. Likewise, almost all ecclesial bodies **had continuity of organization with the Apostolic Church** in that (with the exception of a few Protestant groups) they had the same procedure for admitting Church members—baptism—and celebrated the central Christian service of the eucharist. It may be that we can identify one ecclesial body (or two or more such bodies) as having so much more of such continuity as to deem it (or them) alone to be the Church which Jesus founded. But **maybe** we must say that **the Church is divided**; and that it can only function properly if reunited. Jesus would have recognized that a divine institution can suffer division; the kingdom of Israel, one kingdom under David and Solomon, split in the tenth century BC into the northern kingdom of Israel and the southern kingdom of Judah; and for a time at any rate each recognized the other as part of the same divinely founded state.

Continuity of Doctrine

Because there has been so much agreement between the main ecclesial bodies which survived the disputes of the early centuries about the central theological and moral doctrines of Christianity, there is no need for me, when considering the truth of these doctrines, to face the difficult issue of what are the boundaries of the Church, that is, which one or more ecclesial bodies constitute it. But in order to show these doctrines to be probable overall, I need to show that, in teaching them, the Church was teaching doctrines taught by Jesus or the Apostolic Church or plausible interpretations thereof. From at least the second century onwards the Church had a **generally recognized procedure** (part of what constituted its organization) **about the proper way of deriving doctrines** from the teaching of Jesus and the Apostolic Church, that is, about what constituted continuity of doctrine. Doctrines should be derived from the record of that teaching contained in 'the deposit of faith'. **The deposit of faith** consisted of the Bible (Old Testament and New Testament), often called 'Holy Scripture', and perhaps also, many claimed, of some **unwritten traditions** (the teaching of Jesus and his Apostles not yet committed to writing). (The second Ecumenical Council of Nicaea in AD 787 put the 'unwritten' traditions of the Church on a level with the 'written' ones—that is, with the Bible—when it declared anyone who rejected either tradition to be heretical. But, of course, in order to apply this declaration to some contested issue, it would need to be shown that there was an unwritten tradition on that issue.)

The Origin of the Bible

The **Old Testament** (which also forms the Bible of the Jewish religion) had been put together gradually over many centuries so as to reach more or less its present form by the time of Jesus. And gradually, in the course of the first century AD, the Church came to recognize certain books as containing the essence of the revelation which had been given through Jesus, and these came to form the core of the **New Testament**. The Old Testament was regarded as containing the record of God's gradual earlier revelation, and to be interpreted in the light of the New Testament. So the crucial part of the deposit of faith for the purpose of deriving the teaching of Jesus and the Apostolic Church was the New Testament. The main books of our New Testament were recognized as having this status by the end of the first century. But there was considerable argument for several further centuries about the status of several books, some of which were eventually included (e.g. the Letter to the Hebrews, and the Book of Revelation) and some of which were eventually excluded (e.g. 1 Clement and the Shepherd of Hermas). The first time that anyone listed as canonical (that is, as proper parts of the Bible) exactly the books contained in our present New Testament was in AD 367; and the disputes about which books should be included in the New Testament continued for much longer after that.

What determined which books came to be recognized as canonical? In his book *The Canon of the New Testament* Bruce Metzger analyses **three criteria which led Church bodies to recognize** some book as New Testament Scripture: its conformity with basic Christian tradition, its apostolicity (being written by an Apostle, or someone closely connected with an Apostle), and its widespread acceptance by the Church at large. The ancient document which exhibits most clearly the first two criteria at work is a short work written in the latter part of the second century known as the Muratorian canon. After listing thirteen letters purportedly written by St Paul which he regards as genuine, the author rejects two works that promote a view, which he claimed to be heretical, which he says have been falsely attributed to Paul, because 'it is not fitting that gall be mixed with honey'. He also rejects the Shepherd of Hermas because, although the work 'ought indeed to be read', it was composed 'very recently, in our own times'; and so not an apostolic work. The third criterion—that any given local church ought to recognize a work as Scripture if most others do—is manifest in many later writings.

The first two of Metzger's criteria are criteria of continuity with the original revelation; and the third criterion is the criterion of the recognition of this continuity by other parts of the Church established as such by the criteria (including the organizational criterion) discussed earlier in this chapter. The authority of the Bible thus derives, claimed the early Church, from its recognition by the Church, identified as such by the organizational criterion of continuity as well as by continuity of doctrine in other respects. Although we may need further arguments (additional to those provided in Chapter 8 and to be provided in Chapter 11) to show that the miraculous events associated with the life of Jesus actually occurred, I suggest that my arguments in Chapter 7 suffice to show that the books of the New Testament are basically reliable accounts of the teaching of Jesus and of the Apostolic Church about him. Hence, it is an obvious way of deriving correct doctrines about that teaching, to derive them from the Bible.

There were, however, **often different equally plausible interpretations of biblical passages,** and different interpretations led to different theological doctrines. In that case, the Church held, what **'the Fathers'** said about these interpretations should carry significant weight. 'The Fathers' were the Christian theologians of the early centuries (apart from any subsequently deemed to be heretical); and the more Fathers and the more important Fathers supported one interpretation, the more the weight of opinion favoured that interpretation. But councils of bishops of the Church were recognized as having greater authority, and, as mentioned above, **Ecumenical Councils** of the Church were recognized (by virtually all the Church, from the beginning until the sixteenth century) as having the final say in determining the truth of a disputed doctrine. (As mentioned, this is subject to the qualification that the status of a council as Ecumenical was subsequently given very general recognition; and/or to the qualification that decisions of such councils require the approval of a Pope; and/or to the qualification that the Pope can pronounce infallibly on doctrine without needing prior council approval.) But where there was a virtually unanimous tradition of doctrine on some matter, clearly there was no need for any council decision. And if the doctrine was treated over many centuries in such a way that anyone who denied it would have been deemed heretical and expelled from the Church, then clearly that doctrine would have the same status as one approved by an Ecumenical Council. Such doctrines I will call **central doctrines**. If the Church has God's authority to determine doctrine, and doctrines proposed for consideration constitute plausible interpretations of the deposit of faith, and it uses a method well recognized (by the Church which has this authority) from earliest times for deciding between competing plausible interpretations, then such interpretations will be correct interpretations. I shall argue in Chapter 12 that the Church did derive the Nicene Creed in accord with its own procedures.

But given that doctrines about the teaching and actions of Jesus and the Apostolic Church must be derivable from the Bible (or perhaps from 'unwritten traditions'), the only justification for this would seem to be that **everything in the Bible is true**. The Bible was often described as 'inspired' by God, but no Ecumenical Council ever said anything as precise as that every *sentence* in it was true. And the major reason for that is that it was quite unclear what it would be like for some of its sentences to be true. Everyone for the first 1, 300 years of Christian history thought that the Bible was often difficult to understand—both because it seemed to contain sentences which contradicted other sentences, and also because it seemed to conflict with secular knowledge in the form of Greek science. So before we return to the issue of whether the Church's theological and moral teaching was properly derived from the Bible, we need to examine the rules for interpreting this 'tricky' text, and so to see how far the use of these rules in deriving doctrines commits the Church to the view that everything in the Bible is true.

11 THE BIBLE

The Church has always claimed that the first part of the Bible, the Old Testament, is the record of God's revelation to Israel, and the second part, the New Testament, is the record of God's final revelation through Jesus; and that the Old Testament has to be interpreted in the light of the New. It has claimed that the Bible was inspired by God, although written down by human authors; and so, at any rate when it has a clear message, it is true. I need to discuss this claim, not merely because the Church is committed to the view that doctrine must be derived from the 'deposit of faith', the main (if not the only) part of which is the Bible; but also because the claim seems implausible, and that suggests that the Church cannot be trusted when it defines doctrines. For, objectors claim, scientists and historians have shown that so much in the Bible is false. The world was not created in six days (as Genesis 1 seems to claim); nor was it created in approximately 4000 BC (which is the conclusion you reach if you take literally all the assertions in the Bible about who was who's father and how long they lived); there was no flood which covered the whole earth in 3000 BC (as follows from Genesis 7, given the method of dating just mentioned); and so on.

Genres of Biblical Books

As I noted in the last chapter, the Bible is a big book gradually put together out of many smaller books. These books belong to different *genres*. By the '**genre**' of a book I mean whether it is a work of history (purporting to tell us exactly and literally what happened), a moral fable, a philosophical discussion between imagined participants, or whatever. Whether some sentence or longer passage of a book is to be understood in a literal or metaphorical sense as 'true' or 'false' or neither depends on the genre to which the book belongs. In a modern newspaper report of a battle, or a larger work of **history**, each sentence is (normally) to be understood in a literal sense and can be assessed as 'true' or 'false'. A sentence is true if it describes accurately what happened; false if it does not. The individual sentences of such a work can be assessed separately; and the whole work is more nearly true, the more of its individual sentences are true. We should, however, bear in mind that (as I pointed out in Chapter 5) ancient historians do not have such precise standards of accuracy as modern historians; and so we should judge a sentence of an ancient work of history as true in so far as it satisfied the contemporary standards, for those were the standards which the writer was seeking to satisfy. Augustine commented that minor discrepancies of detail between biblical passages are irrelevant for the purpose of assessing their main historical claims. The Bible contains some works of history, which we can assess for overall truth (if we bear this point in mind). For example, the books of Kings, St Mark's Gospel, and the Acts of the Apostles belong to this genre.

Then the Bible contains a lot of books which I shall call '**historical fables**'. What I mean by a historical fable is a work of literature purportedly based on some main events which happened to real people, but filled out by all sorts of conversations and incidents which the author has imagined and which he is not intending us to take as literally true history. Examples of historical fables include recent television 'docudramas' which tell the main events in the life of Queen Elizabeth I or Julius Caesar, but fill them out in order to illustrate the motives of those involved with conversations which never occurred (and which the author is not claiming did occur). The message of such a work is that the main events described did indeed occur and that the motives of those involved in them were as described. If that message is true, it seems appropriate to call the whole work 'true', but its truth does not depend on the truth of most of its individual sentences, which will in fact be false. Elizabeth said very few of the exact words attributed to her in a typical 'docudrama', and is frequently depicted as meeting people at places where she certainly did not meet them. But that doesn't matter for the truth of the overall message of the play. Many biblical books belong to this genre, for example the book of Judges, the first and second books of Samuel, and (as I suggested in Chapter 7) St John's Gospel.

Then there are **moral fables**, which are fictional stories with a moral message. In my view the books of Daniel and Jonah are moral fables. The book of Daniel is a collection of fictional stories designed to inspire courage to confess faith in God despite persecution. The book of Jonah is a fictional story designed to inspire missionary activity—taking the religion of the Jews to the Gentiles (that is, non-Jews). If we are to assess such a book as 'true' or 'false', all we can mean by saying that the book is 'true' is that its moral message is a true one. Its truth in this sense again does not depend on the truth of its individual sentences. The book of Daniel is true if it is good to confess faith in God despite persecution.

Then the Bible may contain one or more books or parts of books which are what I call '**metaphysical fables**'. These are fictional stories to be understood as metaphors telling us something very important about the human condition. We saw possible examples of such stories in the Gospels (pp. 95–6). The opening chapters of the book of Genesis may also be like this. Genesis 1 may simply be a hymn expressing the dependence of all things on God by means of a story of God creating this on the first day, that on the second day, and so on. But it is disputed whether the author or authors of Genesis 1–3 were attempting to write a historical work or a metaphysical fable. If a metaphysical fable is to be assessed as 'true' or something like that, we must mean by saying that it is true if the human condition is the way that the story, read metaphorically, is claiming. If Genesis 1 is a metaphysical fable, it is true if and only if all things depend on God.

The Bible also contains hymns (the book of Psalms), personal letters (Paul's Letter to Philemon), moral instruction (the book of Proverbs), theological dialogues (the book of Job), and books of many other genres. In many of these cases if it can be said that the book has a 'true' message, its 'truth' does not depend on the truth of its individual sentences.

Difficulties of Modern View of the Truth of the Bible

So how are we to understand the claim that the whole Bible is true? The natural way to understand it is as the claim that each book is true by the criteria of its own genre—that every sentence of a work of history is true (within the limits of accuracy that the author and his culture expected it to satisfy), that the main events of a historical fable did occur, and so on. There are, however, three major difficulties for this way of understanding the Bible, if the Bible is to be used as the Church has claimed that it should be used, as the source of doctrine. The first difficulty is that **we do not know the genre of some biblical books** (and some of them may belong to genres so unfamiliar to us that we do not know what would constitute a book of that genre being 'true'). So we do not know how much of them should be understood in a literal sense. In describing this way of understanding the Bible, I have implicitly and naturally assumed that the genre of a biblical book is determined by the intentions of its original human author and the way it would be understood in the ancient culture for which it was originally written. So whether chapters 1–3 of Genesis are a work of history or a metaphysical fable depends on what the author of these chapters thought he was doing and what the culture who first read them thought he was doing. And we simply do not know that; and that means that we do not know what it is for those chapters to be true. And even if we are right to suppose that these chapters are a metaphysical fable, it is unclear what it means, when understood as a metaphor. And so generally. Even if we think we know the genre of most other biblical books, our views about these matters will sometimes differ from those of most ancient and medieval Christians; and that has the consequence that, if they used the Bible as a source of doctrine, they are likely to have derived false doctrines.

Even when we are concerned with passages of Scripture about whose meaning (understood in the way just outlined) there is little dispute, two substantial difficulties remain. The first is that **there are passages inconsistent with each other**, and so with any Christian doctrine based on one of these passages. The second is that, although some of the apparent clashes with modern knowledge can now be seen as merely apparent—perhaps Genesis 1 is not to be read as saying that the world was made in six days—there remain many **passages inconsistent with the results of modern science and history**. Genesis 5 lists the descendants of Adam, the first man, and claims that they lived for very long periods—Methuselah is said to have lived for 969 years. This part of the early chapters of Genesis is fairly clearly intended to be taken literally. But everything we know about prehistory suggests that humans lived no longer than we do and there was a lot longer chain of descendants of the first human being than Genesis claims.

How the Fathers Interpreted Apparent Falsities

The early Christian theologians were well aware of the difficulties of these two latter kinds. Indeed these difficulties were more acute for them than for us because they were not very sensitive to the existence of different genres, and many theologians tended to assume that the truth of the Bible consisted in every sentence being true. But for many sentences of the Bible they had a different understanding from ours of what it was for those sentences to be true, which enabled them to deal with these difficulties and so to use the Bible as a source of doctrine. The Fathers were well aware that there are **many passages which are inconsistent with what the Fathers believed to be established Christian doctrine**, as stated in other passages. There are passages of the Old Testament which seem inconsistent with a Christian view of the nature of God. Some passages seem to endorse a view of God as vindictive, or pronounce curses on innocent people. One small example is Psalm 137: 9, which pronounces a blessing on those who smash against a rock the children of Babylonians (who had taken Jewish leaders as captives to Babylon). Other passages represent God as too much like an ordinary embodied human being of limited power and knowledge. At the beginning of the third century the highly influential theologian **Origen** commented on one such passage (the Genesis 2–3 story of the garden of Eden):

Who is so silly as to believe that God, after the manner of a farmer 'planted a paradise eastward in Eden', and set in it a visible and palpable 'tree of life' of such a sort that anyone who tasted its fruit with his bodily teeth would gain life? (*On First Principles* 4.3)

There are also, as I commented in the previous chapter, passages in the **New Testament** which, if understood in the most natural literal sense, are **inconsistent with** what the Fathers believed to be **Christian doctrines** derived from other New Testament passages. For example, one passage in Paul's letters which is most naturally understood in a way unfavourable to the doctrine of the Incarnation (that Jesus was God Incarnate) is Paul's claim in his Letter to the Romans (1: 4) that Jesus was 'declared to be Son of God . . . by [his] Resurrection from the dead'.

The precise meaning of the Greek translated here as 'declared to be' is unclear. It may mean 'made' or it may mean 'shown to be'. If we take the former and more normal meaning, the sentence claims that, in consequence of his Resurrection, Jesus acquired a higher status (however 'Son of God' is understood). In that case, Jesus cannot have been always fully divine. But no being not fully divine could become fully divine (in the sense in which all theologians of the fourth century understood being 'divine'); to be God (in the sense of the Creed) is to be eternally God. So this verse taken in isolation suggests that Jesus is not God. If, however, we take the latter meaning, the sentence means that the Resurrection showed us that Jesus had this high status, and that is compatible with his always having had that status. And there are other passages in Paul's letters which certainly imply that Jesus was divine.

Secondly, there are many **biblical passages which seemed inconsistent with the contemporary Greek science**, which the better-educated Fathers often accepted. Thus, Greek science held that the 'natural places' of the four 'elements' were in the form of (roughly) concentric spheres: a spherical earth in the middle of the universe covered by a sphere of water, water by air, air by fire; outside the sphere of fire lay sun, moon, and planets; and finally a solid sphere in which the stars were embedded. The 'firmament' referred to in Genesis 1: 6–8 is then naturally assumed to be this solid sphere. But the Old Testament compares it to a stretched 'skin' (Psalm 104: 2) or to a 'vault', the curved roof of a building (Isaiah 40: 22 in a Latin version); and so to a curved or flat covering to a flat earth, not a sphere. Greek science did not allow there to be water above the 'firmament', as claimed by Genesis 1: 7. And a literal interpretation of the 'days' of creation described in Genesis 1 involved there being 'light' on the first day before the sun, the source of light, was created on the fourth day!

The need to interpret the Bible in a way compatible with Christian doctrine came to be recognized very widely in the early days of the Church. To determine how to interpret Scripture one had to appeal to the ways in which the Fathers and the Church councils had interpreted it in the past (as I explained at the end of the last chapter). Just as which books were to form part of the Bible, so how those books were to be interpreted, was to be determined by a prior understanding of Christian doctrine. At the end of the second century, long before the canon of the New Testament

(the list of books which formed the New Testament) had been
finally agreed, Irenaeus wrote that 'every word' of Scripture 'shall
seem consistent' to someone 'if he for his part diligently read the
Scriptures, in company with those who are presbyters [elders or
priests] in the Church, among whom is the apostolic doctrine'
(*Against Heresies* 4. 32. 1). A few years later the theologian Tertullian
commented that disputes between orthodox and heretics could not
be settled by appeal to Scripture, since its limits and meaning are
uncertain. Scripture belongs to the Church. The Church's teaching
must first be identified and that will determine how Scripture is to
be interpreted. He wrote: 'Wherever it shall be manifest that the
true Christian rule and faith shall be, there will likewise be the true
Scripture and expositions thereof.'

Thus interpretation often involved choosing one rather than
another possible literal meaning (although perhaps a less natural
one) of the text; and so for example, interpreting Romans 1: 4
as saying that Jesus was 'shown to be Son of God . . . by [his]
Resurrection from the dead'.

But sometimes and to varying degrees all the Fathers dealt with
incompatibilities with Christian doctrine adopting by a **radical
metaphorical interpretation of the text**. The passage which I
quoted from Origen continues:

And when God is said to 'walk in the paradise in the cool of the day' and
Adam to hide himself behind a tree, I do not think that anyone will doubt
that these are metaphorical expressions which indicate certain mysteries
by means of a story which does not correspond to actual events.

Among other passages which some of the Fathers interpreted in
this way were accounts of savage or other immoral conduct by
Israelites, and prophecies (for example, in the books of Isaiah or
Ezekiel) that God would avenge the mistreatment of Israel by
various foreign nations (Tyre, Sidon, Egypt, etc.) whose citizens
might not seem to deserve such vengeance.

The Fathers had available to them a whole set of objects
or properties commonly associated with the people, places, and
actions referred to in the Old Testament, which provided symbolic
meanings for the words which normally designated the latter. The
key to understanding the Old Testament, claimed Origen, is the
New Testament teaching of the Kingdom of God as the New

Jerusalem (roughly, Heaven), the Church as the New Israel, Jesus as the new Moses or Joshua, who leads the people of the New Israel to the New Jerusalem in the way that Moses and Joshua led the people of the Old Israel to the 'promised land' of Canaan. Then all Old Testament talk about 'Jerusalem', even if sometimes it can be understood literally as referring to the earthly city of Jerusalem, must be held to have a spiritual reference to the heavenly Jerusalem. So, Origen continues, the prophecies prophesying that God would give different fates to different foreign enemies of Israel are to be understood as prophecies that God would award different fates in the afterlife to different kinds of sinners, who really do have the vices ascribed by the prophecy to the inhabitants of Tyre or Egypt. And although few of the Fathers would interpret the Old Testament in quite such a radical metaphorical way as Origen, many of them gave a metaphorical interpretation to Psalm 137: 9 ('Happy shall they be who take your little ones [the children of Babylon] and dash them against the rock'). Since the Jews became enslaved in Babylon, 'Babylon' comes to represent evil generally; and Jesus had compared relying on him (Jesus) to building one's house on a rock (Matthew 7: 24). Psalm 137: 9 was then interpreted as a blessing on those who take the offspring of evil which are our evil inclinations, and destroy them through the power of Jesus Christ.

Origen's way of treating the Bible was adopted by **Gregory of Nyssa** in the next century, and also (rather more cautiously) by Augustine at the beginning of the fifth century; and it became one standard approach to the Bible. Gregory points out (in the Prologue to his *Commentary on the Song of Songs*) that there is much immoral conduct apparently commended in the Old Testament: 'What benefit to virtuous living can we obtain from the prophet Hosea, or from Isaiah having intercourse with a prophetess, unless something else lies beyond the mere letter?' But the 'mere letter' is only 'the apparent reprehensible sense'; a metaphorical interpretation turns it into 'something having a divine meaning'. **Augustine**'s basic rule was the same as that of Origen and Gregory: 'we must show the way to find out whether a phrase is literal or figurative. And the way is certainly as follows: whatever there is in the word of God that cannot, when taken literally, be referred either to purity of life or soundness of doctrine, you may set down as metaphorical' (*On Christian Doctrine* 9. 10. 14).

Not all the Fathers felt the need to understand any passages incompatible with Greek science in other than the most natural way; some simply held that the literal interpretation of Scripture took precedence over Greek science. But some of them **also interpreted the Bible in the light of Greek science**. Augustine showed in his commentary *The Literal Interpretation of Genesis* that interpreting a passage in accord with 'soundness of doctrine' included interpreting it in accord with educated secular knowledge including Greek science. Much of his commentary was designed to show that Genesis could be understood in literal senses compatible with Greek science, even if not perhaps the most natural literal senses. For example, he argued that perhaps in speaking of the shape of the 'firmament' as a 'vault' Isaiah 'wished to describe that part which is over our head', which looks like a vault to us. Or he suggested maybe the 'firmament' means simply the sky: not the solid sphere postulated by Greek science, but a region of air above which water vapour is as light as air (and so forms the region of 'water above the sky'). But he also felt the need to interpret passages apparently concerned with scientific matters in metaphorical ways. He interpreted the light created on the first day as 'spiritual light', the light which gives to creatures true spiritual understanding. Even so there was the problem of how there could be days before there was a Sun, created according to Genesis on the fourth day. So, like several others of the Fathers, Augustine held that all the things described in Genesis 1 were created simultaneously (as Genesis 2: 4 seems to suggest); and he developed a highly idiosyncratic view that talk about the six 'days' of creation is to be interpreted as talk about stages in the knowledge of creation possessed by the angels.

Even Origen emphasized that **most of the Bible** (and almost all the New Testament) should be understood **in some literal sense**. And almost all the Fathers insisted on literal interpretation of passages more often than he did (although some of them thought that, even when it had a true literal meaning, it had a true metaphorical meaning also). But none of the Fathers would interpret all biblical passages literally, for none of them would interpret the Song of Songs literally—for on its own it is an erotic love poem. They interpreted it in terms of God's love for the Church, the more erotic aspects of which were understood in metaphorical ways.

How the Fathers Justified Their Method of Interpretation

But then what justification did the Fathers have for interpreting passages in ways some of which, it seems clear to us, were not those intended by the original human author? Strangely, their justification for their method of interpretation derives from the very high view of the authority of the Bible which the Fathers had come to hold. In their view **God was the ultimate author of the Bible**, inspiring the human authors to write the biblical books in their own style and with their own limited understanding. Pope Gregory the Great (in the sixth century) described the Bible as 'God's letter to his creature'. It follows that the text should be interpreted in the light of God's beliefs, not those of the human authors; and of the beliefs of the community for which the Fathers believed the Bible was intended, the whole human race, and not merely those who first read it. And 'the human race' must be understood as the human race of future as well as past centuries.

It is a basic rule for interpreting all texts that you interpret them in a way consistent with the author's known beliefs (unless you have some reason to suppose that he is trying to deceive his readers, which is ruled out in this case by the perfect goodness of God) and the beliefs which he believes that his audience (or at least many of them) hold. Suppose I say to you about someone that 'he has a sharp brain'. Since I know and I know that you know that brains are not the sort of thing that have sharp edges, what I say cannot be understood as saying that 'he' has a brain with a sharp edge. So I must be understood to be saying something else which the sentence could mean. I must mean that he has a sharp intelligence; he can recognize distinctions and draw consequences. Yet if I thought and thought that you thought that brains were the sort of thing which can have either blunt or sharp edges, what I said would have quite a different meaning. And if someone utters a sentence which clearly neither he nor his hearers believe if understood in any literal sense, it must be understood metaphorically. We consider if the sentence would be an appropriate thing for the speaker to have said if some word in it did not pick out the thing it normally picks out, but rather some feature believed by the speaker and his hearers to be associated with that thing. If it would be an appropriate thing to

say if so understood, then that is what it means. If I describe some
person John, whom we all know to be human, as a 'dinosaur', that
cannot be understood literally. So I must be saying that John has
some feature believed to be possessed by dinosaurs, e.g. the fact that
the dinosaurs could not adapt quickly to a change of environment
and so died out. I am saying that John cannot change his way
of thinking and behaving, and that people like him will soon no
longer exist.

God knows the truths of Christian doctrine and the truths of
science and history. The Fathers believed that the Church knows at
the least most of the truths of Christian doctrine; and they believed
that they themselves knew most of the truths of science and history.
They did, however, admit that not all truths of Christian doctrine
had yet been derived from the deposit of faith; and they allowed
the possibility that future generations might discover more about
science and history than they knew themselves. But, they claimed,
the Bible must be interpreted in the light of what they did know
about these matters; and hence the way they interpreted passages
apparently inconsistent with Christian doctrine or science and
history. So if some passage understood in the most natural literal
sense is inconsistent with some item of Christian doctrine (itself
derived from some other passage of Scripture), we should interpret
it so as to be consistent with that item, even if that is not the most
natural interpretation of the passage taken in isolation. And if some
passage, understood in its most natural literal sense, is inconsistent
with some manifest truth of science or history, it is also inconsistent
with something that God knows, and so to be understood in some
less natural way.

This has the consequence that the human author may have
written some passage which he understood in one way but which
God intended to be taken in another and deeper way. The Fathers
generally supposed that the human author understood what he was
writing in the correct sense; but they allowed the possibility that
prophets might sometimes not understand the prophecies which
they were given, from which it follows that **the human authors of
biblical books** (who were often described as 'prophets') **did not
always understand** how their works were to be understood.

The Fathers may seem to us correct in interpreting passages
of Scripture capable of two fairly natural interpretations (as in
the example of Romans 1: 4) in ways compatible with what the

Church deemed to be true Christian doctrine. Jesus did not write a book but founded a Church with the task of interpreting doctrines (including ones committed to writing) for new generations. Yet the highly metaphorical way in which some of the Fathers read the Old Testament seems quite unnatural to us. But they lived in a cultural atmosphere where **large-scale allegory seemed very natural**; it was a very familiar genre in terms of which it was natural to interpret any passage which you did not think could be understood literally. The Jewish philosopher Philo in the first century BC had already given a highly allegorical interpretation of Genesis and other Old Testament books. Several commentators of classical and later Greece even interpreted the narrative poems of Homer, the *Iliad* and the *Odyssey*, which told the story of the Trojan war and of Odysseus' return to Ithaca, allegorically. Metrodorus of Lampsacus interpreted the heroes and heroines of the *Iliad* as items of astronomy and physics: Agamemnon as the ether, Achilles as the Sun, Helen as the earth, etc., and so interpreted the *Iliad* as a scientific treatise!

What Origen and Gregory were doing was to understand a lot of the Old Testament in the way in which we and Bunyan himself interpret John Bunyan's book *The Pilgrim's Progress*. This is the story of a pilgrim named 'Christian' journeying to 'the Heavenly City', and this journey clearly corresponds to what Bunyan claims to be the gradual formation of a typical Christian's character by doing actions so as to make him fitted for Heaven. There are obstacles and diversions making the journey a difficult one, and these (in view of the similarities between physical obstacles on a path, and temptations making it difficult for someone to pursue a goal with constancy) correspond to the temptations which beset the Christian in his life. Thus, after beginning his journey, Christian comes to a mire, the Slough of Despond, through which he must pass. Struggling in the mire at the beginning of his journey corresponds to the situation of the sinner when, 'awakened about his lost condition, there ariseth in his soul many fears, and doubts, and discouraging apprehensions'. For the first part of his journey Christian has to bear on his back a heavy burden, of which he cannot rid himself, but which falls from his back when he comes to a cross. The guilt of our sin is thus compared to a burden of which we cannot rid ourselves, but of which Christ rids us through his death on the Cross. And so on.

The Nicene Creed's doctrine that **God the Holy Spirit 'spake by the prophets'** clearly entailed the **doctrine that God 'inspired' the writing of the Old Testament**; and it soon naturally enough came to be understood as the doctrine that God inspired the writing of the whole of the Bible. This doctrine allows the view that the inspiration affected only the clear messages of biblical passages and not the detailed ways in which those messages were spelled out. All the same, is it plausible to suppose that God 'inspired' the writing of savage prophecies against Tyre and Sidon, let alone the blessing on those who smash the heads of the children of Babylon—even if a later generation could derive a deeply religious message from this? The answer must be that even these prophecies and blessings understood in their original sense contain a small amount of truth, one so obvious to us that we do not notice it, but not at all obvious to those with very little moral sensitivity. Mercy is often better than justice; but mercy is letting people off the just punishment which they deserve. You cannot have a concept of mercy unless you have a prior concept of justice. The people of Tyre and Sidon had hurt Israel, and deserved to be punished, even if it would be better to show them mercy. And the parents of the children of Babylon had wronged Israel and so they deserved punishment, and punishing their children would be punishing them; but, of course, the children did not deserve any punishment, let alone that punishment implied by Psalm 139. And later parts of the Old Testament asserted that children should not be punished for the sins of their parents: 'A child shall not suffer for the iniquity of a parent, nor a parent suffer for the iniquity of a child,' wrote the prophet Ezekiel (18: 20). It is plausible to suppose that God inspired the writing of a book some parts of which have a highly inadequate morality which is capable of being understood as time progressed in a far deeper way. And the same goes for the passages which express doctrines with false scientific presuppositions: the Genesis 1 account of creation taught the true message that the existence of the inanimate world, plants, animals, and humans depended on God alone, even if it gave a false picture of the method and timescale. Later science would sort out the latter. And so many of the apparently historical stories have obvious morals, even if they have no basis in history. Whether or not Israel really worshipped a Golden Calf and was punished by Moses for doing so (Exodus 32), everyone who hears the story can learn that no material object deserves worship. Small children today as well as ancient Israelites get simple messages from simple stories. So I suggest that it is plausible to suppose that, whether indirectly through the natural forces which developed the religious sensitivity of its human authors or by a more direct intervention into their conscious life, God inspired the writing of the Bible, to convey both the very limited message comprehensible at the time a passage was written and the deeper message comprehensible later.

These principles of biblical interpretation allowed the Fathers to interpret quite a lot of the Bible without needing to know the genre of the biblical book or exactly what the original human writer meant. Hence, just as the Fathers could deal with the second and third difficulties for the modern way of interpreting the Bible mentioned above, so they could deal with the first difficulty also. If there was an obvious literal sense compatible with Christian doctrine and with science and history, that was the sense of the passage. And while a prior understanding of Christian doctrine often determined the sense of the passage, often it did not; and so it could then be interpreted in the natural literal sense and be used for deriving new doctrines. If, however, the passage had to be interpreted metaphorically, it was often unclear what the metaphor was and so how it should be interpreted. And there were many disagreements about how passages should be interpreted, and frequently many of the Fathers admitted that they couldn't understand quite a bit of the Bible.

Origen, Gregory, and Augustine lived during the period in which the Church was deciding which books belonged to the Bible and which did not; and it is very doubtful whether we would have today's Bible without that Church's general recognition of their way of understanding it as a permissible way of understanding it. Origen was the most influential Christian theologian subsequent to St Paul; and although after his death suspected of heresy for reasons having nothing to do with the way in which he interpreted Scripture, his influence in this latter respect was profound. Gregory of Nyssa was one of the leading bishops of the Council of Constantinople which approved the Nicene Creed, including its claim that the Holy Spirit 'spoke by the prophets', and Augustine was the theologian who influenced the development of theology in the West far more than any other early theologian. This tradition of interpretation was common to much subsequent biblical interpretation both in the East and in the West. A discussion of the rules of biblical interpretation widely influential in the West was the twelfth-century Hugh of St Victor's *Didascalion*. 'Sacred Scripture', Hugh wrote, 'has three ways of conveying meaning—namely history, allegory, and tropology.' By 'allegory' in the narrow sense in which he uses the term in this paragraph, Hugh understands a metaphorical interpretation conveying Christian doctrine; by 'tropology' he understands a metaphorical interpretation conveying moral instruction. 'To be sure,' he continues, 'all things in the divine utterance must not be wrenched to an interpretation such that each of them is held to contain history, allegory, and tropology all at once,' as some had taught. There are, he asserts firmly, certain places in the divine page which cannot be read literally (*Didascalion* 5. 2 and 6. 4).

When the Church recognized the authority of the Bible, it gave us at the same time a method for interpreting it. There is no justification for taking the one without the other. The Protestant Reformation, however, largely rejected this tradition. Many Protestants claimed that they could understand the Bible simply by reading it, and derive all Christian doctrine from it without any prior assumptions about the content of doctrine, or even any historical knowledge of the original genres of biblical books. But, as I have emphasized, there are biblical passages which, taken in their most natural literal sense, are incompatible with other passages. Without some prior understanding of Christian doctrine, there is no way of resolving these incompatibilities. If all Christians had been killed and almost all their books burnt in the Roman persecutions, and then a thousand years later a Bible had been discovered buried in the sands of Egypt and some scholar had tried to derive from the Bible an account of what Christians believed about the nature of God, it seems to me immensely unlikely that he would have come up with the doctrine of the Trinity. And if the Bible is all that you have to rely on, you will take passages which are not in conflict with other passages in their most natural literal senses; and that leads straight to the immensely implausible doctrine of a universe only 6,000 years old. If you have a tradition of interpreting in the light of known science, you will avoid that.

As I mentioned above, the Fathers of the Church who accepted the achievements of Greek science were not committed to the view that there was no more science to be discovered. So if we are to interpret the Bible by their method **we must interpret it in a way compatible with modern science (and history) as well as with established Christian doctrine**. Interestingly this tradition of interpretation is going to yield many of the same results about the genres of biblical books as those reached by a modern understanding (described earlier) of the circumstances in which those books were written. When Old Testament scholars realized that the book of Daniel was written, not as it seems to claim in the sixth century BC but in the second century BC, they realized that its purpose was to inspire courage in the face of persecution by means of fictional stories of such courage being shown in the face of sixth-century persecution. Hence it belongs (in my terminology) to the genre of moral fable. If the Fathers had realized that its content was not history, they would have said that it should be interpreted in much the same way. But their grounds would not have been those provided by evidence of the human author's intention and the way the book would have been understood by its first readers; but merely by the fact that, taken as literal history, it was false. But the Fathers' method of interpreting the Bible yields a different result from the modern method with respect to any parts of the Bible which were written as history (e.g. Genesis 5) but were in fact false—the events never happened. The modern method would count such passages as false; the method of the Fathers would lead us to read them in some metaphorical way (compatible with Christian doctrine) and count them as true.

The consequence of their method of reading the Bible is that, although the Bible contains much with a clear meaning which can be used for the development of further doctrine, and for spelling out theologically the consequences of existing doctrine, it contains nothing false unless the presupposition of this way of interpreting it—the truth of central Christian doctrines—is itself false. But like many poems, the Bible has more than one meaning. Even if the Church is correct in understanding the Bible as being a divinely inspired book when we understand it in the way which I have just described, it is clearly also a collection of books written by human authors, some of which they and their contemporaries understood as having a different meaning. Indeed, in order to establish the probable truth of Christian doctrines quite a lot of the New Testament has to be understood in the sense appropriate to the genre of its books, understood merely as books written by human authors for their contemporaries, in the way indicated in Chapters 7 and 8. We cannot assume the authority of the Bible interpreted sometimes in a unfamiliar way until we have established it on the basis of the historical evidence provided by certain parts of it understood in a familiar way. But when we have done that, if we are to follow Church tradition in using the Bible as the authoritative source of doctrine, we must also follow Church tradition in the method by which we interpret it.

12 FINAL CONCLUSION

The Church's Teaching

I came to the conclusion in Chapter 9 that, on the evidence of the life and teaching of Jesus (and, I added in Chapter 10, the teaching of the Apostolic Church about him), it is very probable that Jesus was God Incarnate. But what happened afterwards is also relevant evidence. We have seen that, if God became incarnate for the purposes described, he would need to found a Church which he would ensure would continue his work, report his actions, and interpret his teaching for new cultures and generations. So we need evidence that the Church founded by Jesus subsequently provided plausible interpretations of his actions and teaching and the teaching of the Apostolic Church about him, and that these interpretations constitute plausibly true doctrines. I repeat that I am using the word 'plausible' in the sense defined earlier, as 'not very improbable'. A major point of the later Church is to draw out the implications of the teaching of God Incarnate for later cultures and generations when these are not too obvious. So if we have good evidence that God has put his signature on the Church's teaching, its interpretations do not already have to be very probably true interpretations before we reasonably believe them (that is, before they are probable overall). But if the Church's interpretations were not even plausible, that would cast serious doubt on whether God had put his signature on the Church's teaching. And similarly, even if they are plausible interpretations of the teaching of Jesus and the Apostolic Church, the Church's subsequent interpretations must themselves constitute plausibly true doctrines; but they need not (all) be already probable on grounds other than that the Church taught them. For again the point of a revelation is to tell us things for which we do not otherwise have adequate evidence. (But clearly those doctrines which report the evidence for the Church's authority (for example, that Jesus rose from the dead) must be already probable on other grounds.)

Later Church doctrines Are Plausible Interpretations of the Teaching of Jesus and the Apostolic Church

In Chapter 10 I analysed what constituted the Church which Jesus founded; and it follows that either in an integrated or divided form that Church undoubtedly exists today. I pointed out that from the early second century onwards the Church considered that for Christian doctrines to constitute plausible interpretations of the teaching of Jesus and the Apostolic Church, they must be derived from the deposit of faith, primarily the Bible. There may, however, be rival interpretations of this teaching which are also plausible. In order for a plausible interpretation to become a central doctrine, it must, if contested, be given subsequent approval by an Ecumenical Council widely recognized as such by the Church almost everywhere and over many centuries (and/or, in the view of some, the approval of the Pope). This condition (including the Pope's approval) is satisfied for all the doctrines of the Nicene Creed.

These doctrines were derived from passages of the New Testament in the way outlined at the end of Chapter 10 (and filled out in Chapter 11). **For most of these doctrines there were no apparently contradictory passages in the New Testament**, and most of them were not the subject of controversy at any stage before they reached the Creed. I argued earlier that Jesus assumed the doctrine of God as creator, and taught that he (Jesus) was making atonement for our sins, that he would come again in judgement, that the dead would be raised—the good rewarded with Heaven, and the bad facing Hell (in the sense and with the limits described earlier)—and that he was founding a Church whose entrance ceremony was baptism 'for the forgiveness of sins'. And the Apostolic Church taught about Jesus that he suffered, was crucified (and so died), and was buried, rose from the dead, and ascended into Heaven. New Testament passages support these doctrines, and there are no conflicting passages. All of these doctrines were taught in the Church for the next two centuries, virtually without exception. There were from time to time those who claimed that Jesus did not suffer or die on the Cross; what suffered was a mere 'image' of Jesus. This latter doctrine, known as 'docetism', was soon deemed heretical by the vast majority of the

Church, and it is not one likely to seem plausible to any modern enquirer.

The doctrine of the Virgin Birth is also derivable from the New Testament (Matthew 1: 18 and Luke 1: 34–5), and, as I commented in Chapter 7, there are not any obvious contradictory passages in the New Testament. The fact of it appearing in two very different New Testament sources leads us to conclude that it was taught fairly widely in the Apostolic Church, whether or not unanimously we cannot tell. This doctrine was generally accepted in the Church from the second century onwards; the one group who did not accept it was the Jewish–Christian sect of the Ebionites. It was not in dispute at any Church councils, and there was no hesitation in incorporating it into Nicene Creed.

There are, however, **two central doctrines**, indeed the two subsequently most important of all Christian doctrines, **with respect to which there are conflicting New Testament passages. The first such doctrine is that of the divinity of Jesus.** I have already argued in Chapter 7 that some things that Jesus said entail this doctrine. The doctrine is stated clearly and explicitly in three New Testament books: John's Gospel, the book of Revelation, and the Letter to the Hebrews. It is also there in my view in several passages in Paul's letters. One of these passages is Philippians 2: 6–11, which may be a hymn used in the Church and incorporated by Paul into his letter. This speaks of 'Christ Jesus, who though he was in the form of God did not regard equality with God as something to be exploited, but emptied himself, taking the form of a slave being born in human likeness'.

There are, however, as I noted in the previous chapter, passages in the New Testament which, taken in isolation in their most natural sense, seem to deny this doctrine. But the substantial positive assertions in the New Testament of the divinity of Jesus, and, above all, the reasons which I have given for supposing that Jesus himself taught his divinity meant that the Church had already existing doctrine which led it to interpret those awkward passages in ways determined by that doctrine. Second- and third-century Christians generally taught that Jesus was in some way divine (though in what way was somewhat unclear), but there was again the exception of the Jewish–Christian sect of the Ebionites, who denied it. The issue was brought to a head in the fourth century by Arius, who also in effect denied it; and it was in condemnation of the view of Arius and his followers that in AD 325 the Council of Nicaea firmly insisted that Jesus, the Son, was 'of the same essence' as the Father, a view repeated in the Nicene Creed. Arianism gradually died out, and the divinity of Christ became the virtually universal view of Christendom for the next 1,600 years.

The second doctrine relevant to which there are conflicting New Testament passages **is the doctrine of the Trinity**. As I wrote in Chapter 7, it is undisputed that Jesus did not teach this doctrine explicitly; and I have argued that there was good reason why, even if he believed this doctrine, he would not do so. But I also pointed out that the Gospels contain a few sayings of Jesus which provided the later Church with material to develop that doctrine. The doctrine is also implicit in some of the teaching of the Apostolic Church. The synoptic Gospels see the Spirit as a separate agent from the Father and the Son, operating not merely in the baptism and temptation of Jesus but also at his birth; Acts 2 records the descent of the Spirit on the Church after the Resurrection, and there is much about the Spirit elsewhere in Acts and in Paul's letters and in the book of Revelation. The New Testament also contains one or two formulae of a Trinitarian kind, e.g. the last verse of 2 Corinthians: 'The grace of the Lord Jesus Christ, the love of God, and the communion of the Holy Spirit be with you all.' But the New Testament contains nowhere anything like a full doctrine of the Trinity; and the same passages which taken in their most natural sense imply that Jesus is not divine count against the doctrine that he belonged to a divine Trinity.

While most theologians of the second and third centuries believed in a divine trinity of some kind, some of them believed in a trinity of 'modes', different ways in which God manifested his presence, rather than a trinity of individuals or persons. At the beginning of the third century Origen taught that the Trinity was a trinity of individuals, and this view was taken forward by a group of fourth-century theologians, known as the Cappadocians (Basil of Caesarea, Gregory Nazianzen, and Gregory of Nyssa), who claimed that God was one essence (*ousia*) in three individuals (*hypostases*). These latter theologians were responsible for the Nicene Creed's formula that the Spirit is to be jointly worshipped and glorified with the Father and the Son. This doctrine more than any other doctrine of the Creed was clearly a development of ideas at most implicit in the teaching of Jesus. Gregory Nazianzen, who, as archbishop of Constantinople, presided at the opening session of the Council of Constantinople, which approved the Nicene Creed containing this doctrine, was well aware that its formulation was the result of a long process of development; and he gave this explanation (in the same spirit as the one which I have given) of why such a long process was necessary:

You will reach perfection only by continuing to expand. For example, the Old Testament proclaimed the Father openly, the Son more obscurely. The New Testament has clearly shown the Son but only suggested the divinity of the Spirit. In our day the Spirit lives among us and gives us a clear indication of himself. For it was not without danger when the divinity of the Father was not yet confessed, to proclaim the Son openly; nor when the divinity of the Son was not yet admitted to add on the Holy Spirit as a burden, to use a somewhat audacious term. Otherwise, weighed down, so to speak, by the nourishment that was too much for them and looking up into the sun with eyes still too weak, humans risked losing even what they had. (*Oration* 31. 26)

As with the doctrine of the divinity of Jesus, the continuity is there; but there is a much weaker base for this doctrine in the New Testament. However, the interpretation of the New Testament texts is (in my sense) a plausible one, even if there are equally plausible rival interpretations.

As I wrote earlier, the Council of Constantinople was recognized as having ecumenical status by virtually all surviving ecclesial bodies for the next thousand years. Hence its determination of which interpretations of the deposit of faith were the correct ones and so **the Council's approval of the Nicene Creed must constitute the Church's final approval of that**.

The moral doctrines of Christianity which I set out in Chapter 5 were never formulated in a creed approved by a council; and the reason for that is that they were never seriously disputed by any significant body of Church opinion. The obligation to keep the Ten Commandments, but to do more by way of worshipping God, feeding, clothing, and sheltering other humans, and preaching the Christian Gospel to them, clearly contained in the New Testament, was universally recognized for most of the subsequent 2,000 years as central Christian doctrine. For this reason it did not need the approval of an Ecumenical Council in order to have the same permanent status as one so approved. For reasons of space I shall not discuss further the more detailed moral teaching which I mentioned in Chapter 5, concerned primarily with family matters (divorce, sexual intercourse outside marriage, abortion, etc.). Clearly this detailed filling-out of what is involved in the Christian duty of loving God and loving one's neighbour is not quite as important as the duty of love itself. But it has always been regarded as an important element of Christian teaching; and fairly evidently much of it is contained in the teaching of Jesus and the Apostolic Church.

The Later Church's Teachings Constitute Plausible Doctrines

The final requirement that Jesus needs to satisfy if he is to be God incarnate is that the doctrines which the later Church derives from the teaching of Jesus and the Apostolic Church must be themselves plausible (that is, not very improbable) independently of their having been taught by the later Church. I have already argued in Chapter 9 that, if the existence of God has a moderate prior probability (to give it an artificially precise value: of $\frac{1}{4}$ or even somewhat less than that), then when we take into account the historical evidence about the life, teaching, and Resurrection of Jesus (and the teaching of the Apostolic Church about him), **many of these doctrines are not merely plausible but probable (on evidence other than the fact that they were taught by the later Church)**. It is probable that there is a God, and so (by the arguments of Chapter 2) God who is a Trinity. It was to be expected (either certainly or quite probably) that God would become incarnate to do certain things. There is only one serious candidate for being God incarnate about whom there is historical evidence to be expected if he did these things and not in the least to be expected if he did not. So, I argued in Chapter 9, it is very probable that God became incarnate in Jesus, who led a perfect life, suffered, was crucified, and buried; and that he rose from the dead, made atonement for our sins, and founded a Church. Given that Jesus was God Incarnate, it follows that (given the initial plausibility of this teaching, for which I argued in Part I) what he taught about God and morality is true: it would have been wrong to teach false doctrines on these matters and (I argued in Chapter 3) God would have become incarnate in such a way as not to allow him to do wrong. It is not open to serious dispute that Jesus taught that God would at some future time bring this world order to an end, and permanently separate the good and bad in the afterlife. Nor is it open to serious dispute that he (or the Apostolic Church which expounded his teaching) gave much of the moral teaching which I argued to be plausible in Chapter 5. So the historical evidence already makes all of these doctrines not merely plausible but probable.

There are, however, **two or more doctrines that are no more than plausible** (not very improbable) **on evidence other than that they were taught by the later Church**. These may include the doctrines about **which member of the Trinity was the primary agent of what**; e.g. that it is the Son (in the sense of 'Son' explained in Chapter 2) who became incarnate. But clearly, given that there are only three members of the Trinity, any claim about who does which of the jobs done by God are going to be at least plausible. Then there is the doctrine that **God 'spake by the prophets'** (in the sense that God inspired the writing of every biblical book). I gave reasons in Chapter 11 for thinking this doctrine plausible, but some readers may feel that it cannot be regarded as more probable than that on evidence other than that it was taught by the later Church. Then there is one historical doctrine mentioned in the Creed which to my mind is not overall probable on the historical evidence (set out in Chapters 7 and 8). This is the doctrine of the **Virgin Birth**. While, I claimed, for God to bring about the incarnation by means of a virgin birth would be a natural way of symbolizing the doctrine of the Incarnation, it cannot be said to have a very high prior probability. There is certainly, I suggested in Chapter 7, some historical evidence (in the claims of two Gospels derived from independent traditions) which is of a kind to be expected if the Virgin Birth occurred (and not otherwise). But maybe it is not much more probable that we would have this evidence if the doctrine were true than if it were false: the evidence is not very strong. Still, I suggest, it is sufficient in the light of the a priori reason, to make the doctrine at least plausible in my sense. So, I claim, the final requirement which a prophet's life needs to satisfy if it is to be the life of God Incarnate, that, not merely should the Church which he founded give plausible interpretations of his teaching, but the content of those interpretations should be plausibly true, is satisfied by Jesus and the Church which he founded.

But, given the evidence that Jesus founded a Church and that a major purpose of this was to provide a means through which God would ensure that future generations had available a correct account of the teaching of Jesus and of what was important in his life, I claimed that **God will provide the Church with guidance to ensure that what it teaches as central doctrine over many centuries is true**. Hence, given all the other evidence for Jesus being God Incarnate and founding a Church to continue his work, any doctrine of the Creed which is not probable (in the sense of 'more probable than not'), but merely plausible on evidence independent of the Church's teaching, is made probable by the fact of its being taught by the Church (over many centuries over the whole Church as central doctrine). So I conclude that all the doctrines of the Creed (including any which are merely plausible on the historical evidence about Jesus) are overall probable (when we take into account the Church's virtually unanimous teaching over very many centuries).

I illustrate this pattern of argument by an **analogy** in which A represents Jesus (and the Apostolic Church) and B represents the later Church. Suppose that initially we have good evidence that some person A provides totally reliable teaching about all the events of his life and the people with whom he interacted, evidence which includes evidence about the reliability of those people as witnesses. Suppose that this evidence includes evidence that he taught that some disciple B could be trusted to give a correct account of A's teaching and its implications. Then the very fact that B taught that A taught or implied that so-and-so provides good evidence for believing that so-and-so. But the evidence is only good enough to make it probable (more probable than not) that so-and-so, so long as it is plausible (not very improbable) that A taught or implied that so-and-so, and also plausible that so-and-so. If it is not plausible that A taught or implied that so-and-so (e.g. because we have other knowledge of what A taught which makes it very improbable that he taught or implied that so-and-so), or (whether or not A taught it) it is implausible that so-and-so, that provides evidence against so-and-so, and so also evidence against A being a person who provides totally reliable teaching. Why only 'plausibility' is required here and not 'probability' (that is, being 'more probable than not') is because the mere fact that we are told that so-and-so by B, about whose reliability as a witness we already have good evidence, gives us good grounds for believing it anyway. If we needed it to be probable (on evidence other than the testimony of B) that so-and-so or that A said that so-and-so before we had good grounds to believe B when he tells us that so-and-so, then the fact that we are told this by B would be irrelevant.

My claim is that it is only for the doctrines of the Virgin Birth, and perhaps the doctrine of the divine inspiration of the Bible (and perhaps also for doctrines about which member of the Trinity was the primary agent of which divine action), that we need the fact of their incorporation into the Creed to make it probable (more probable than not) that they are true. But given that there is a significant prior probability of the existence of God, and that the historical evidence about the life and Resurrection of Jesus which was God's signature on his teaching (and that of the Apostolic Church) is as strong as I represented it, **any other doctrine taught by the Church** (over many centuries over the whole Church as central doctrine) **will be made much more probable by the very fact of its being taught by the Church**. The Nicene Creed is just such a statement of Christian doctrine. So if some other doctrine of the Creed which was not evidently and explicitly taught by Jesus (or the Apostolic Church), for example, the doctrine of the Trinity, was not quite as probable as—I claim—my a priori arguments suggest, then it would still be made probable by the fact of its incorporation in the Creed. But if some such doctrine was a priori not merely improbable but very improbable (that is, implausible) on other grounds (or it did not constitute a plausible interpretation of the teaching of Jesus or the Apostolic Church), then that would make it improbable that Jesus founded a Church with divine authority to interpret his teaching and actions, and that in turn would greatly reduce the probability that the Resurrection occurred. But given that the doctrine of the Trinity and any other doctrine which does not seem a priori quite as probable as I have claimed is at least plausible (and given that it is at least a plausible interpretation of the teaching of Jesus or the Apostolic Church), then the very fact of its having been incorporated into the Creed makes it probable that it is true.

I conclude that the fact that the later Church taught the other items of the Nicene Creed in no way detracts from the very probable truth of the central claim of the Nicene Creed (made, I have claimed, very probable on other grounds) that Jesus was God (that is, a divine person). From that it follows, since no divine person can cease to be divine, that **Jesus is God**.

INDEX